April, 2025

Mastering Generative AI

A Practical Guide to Machine Learning and Deep Learning

Mr. Rakesh Kumar

Copyright © 2025 by Mr. Rakesh Kumar

ISBN: 979-82813832-6-4

Dedication

To my dearest patient, **Father Kartik Ram** and **Mother Punni Devi**, whose strength and perseverance taught me the true meaning of resilience.
To my loving spouse, **Shakuntala**, whose unwavering support continues to light my path.
And to my friends, who believed in me when it mattered most.
This book is as much yours as it is mine.

Preface

Mastering Generative AI: A Practical Guide to Machine Learning and Deep Learning is a comprehensive and authoritative guide that delves into the foundational principles, methodologies, and real-world applications of Generative AI—a rapidly advancing field that is transforming industries in the digital age.

The book begins with an overview of Generative AI, tracing its evolution and exploring its key applications, challenges, and ethical implications. It lays a solid groundwork by introducing essential machine learning concepts, enabling readers to grasp the underpinnings of AI models and their learning mechanisms. The discussion then transitions into deep learning, highlighting its pivotal role in advancing Generative AI. Topics such as neural network architectures, optimization techniques, and training methodologies are covered in depth.

A core focus of the book is on state-of-the-art Generative AI techniques, including Variational Autoencoders (VAEs), Generative Adversarial Networks (GANs), Transformers, and Diffusion Models. Each technique is thoroughly explained, with an emphasis on its role in contemporary AI research and its practical applications.

The book also explores the intersection of machine learning and generative modeling, discussing hybrid systems and cutting-edge approaches to synthetic data generation. Ethical and security considerations are examined in detail, addressing critical issues such as algorithmic bias, misinformation, intellectual property rights, and the need for regulatory frameworks.

Concluding with forward-looking insights, the book considers emerging trends and the future trajectory of Generative AI, including developments toward Artificial General Intelligence (AGI) and autonomous AI agents.

Written for researchers, professionals, and students alike, this book is an essential resource for anyone seeking a deep and structured understanding of Generative AI and its transformative potential across diverse domains.

Table of Content

Acknowledgments

I would like to express my heartfelt gratitude to everyone who stood by me throughout the creation of this book.

To my **spouse**, thank you for your unwavering support, patience, and encouragement during every late night and early morning spent writing.

To my **friends**, your constant motivation and belief in my abilities kept me going even when the path wasn't easy.

A special thanks to my **patient**, whose strength and determination inspired me more than words can say.

I'm also grateful to the **technical community** and tools that made my research and writing smoother, and to the countless developers, writers, and innovators who continue to shape the world of AI and ML.

Lastly, I thank **you, the reader**, for choosing this book. May it inspire you to explore, learn, and grow in the fascinating world of Generative AI, Machine Learning and Deep Learning.

CHAPTER 1: INTRODUCTION TO GENERATIVE AI

Learning Objective

This chapter introduces Generative AI, tracing its evolution and differentiating it from Discriminative AI. It explores various applications, ethical considerations, and provides a concise overview of AI fundamentals. Readers will gain a foundational understanding of Generative AI's significance and role in modern technology.

1.1   What is Generative AI?

Generative artificial intelligence, or GenAI, is a technology that lets user create new content—text, photographs, videos, sounds, code, 3D designs, and more—by responding to a range of signals. It is taught and "learns" using existing online materials and artefacts.

As generative AI continues to learn from additional data, it develops. Large unlabelled data sets are used to train AI models and algorithms, which are created using sophisticated mathematics and a lot of processing power. These datasets teach the AI to forecast results in a manner similar to what people would do or produce on their own.

The proliferation of generative AI may be attributed in large part to the fact that individuals can now prompt AI using natural language, expanding its range of applications. AI generators are now being utilised as a writing, research, coding, design, and other companion tool across several sectors.

1. Types of Generative AI

There are many distinct kinds of generative AI, each with special traits and uses. The three main categories into which these models fall are as follows:

a) **Transformer-Based Models:** Transformer-based models like GPT-3 and GPT-4 have proved crucial for text generation. They are able to create very coherent and contextually relevant language because of their design, which takes into account the input text's whole context.

b) **Generative Adversarial Networks (GANs):** A discriminator and a generator are the two components that make up a GAN. New data instances are produced by the generator, and their authenticity is assessed by the discriminator. In essence, the two components play a game in which the discriminator tries to improve at identifying the phoney data while the generator tries to produce data that the discriminator cannot tell apart from the genuine data. The generator gains proficiency in producing very lifelike data instances over time.

c) **Variational Autoencoders (VAEs):** Another kind of generative model that makes use of statistical inference concepts is the VAE. To create new data, they first encode input data into a latent space,

which is a compressed representation of the data,
and then they decode this latent representation.
Incorporating a randomness element into the
encoding process enables VAEs to produce data
instances that are both varied and comparable.

There are additional models, but transformer-based
models, VAEs, and GANs are some of the most widely
used generative AI models at the moment. Normalising
flow models, which use a sequence of transformations to
explain complicated data distributions, and autoregressive
models, which forecast future data points based on past
ones, are two deserving of attention.

2. Technologies and Concepts Powering Generative AI

The operation of generative AI tools is made possible by a
number of basic concepts and technologies:

a) Neural Networks and Deep Learning

These are the fundamental components of generative
artificial intelligence. Machines can identify patterns and
correlations in data thanks to neural networks, which
mimic how the human brain processes information.

Neural networks with many layers that are capable of
learning hierarchical representations are used in deep
learning. This makes it possible to create intricate and
subtle information using a variety of data formats,
including text, images, and sound.

b) Transformers

Transformers are sophisticated models that aid in comprehending human language context. This is referred to as natural language processing.

The developments in transformers, which allow these AI tools to quickly produce logical and contextually appropriate text as answers to human enquiries, excite many new users of programs like ChatGPT.

c) Variational Autoencoders (Vaes)

VAEs are similar to painters in that they study a number of paintings before producing new works in the same style. They may create new objects that look like the originals after learning the substance of the data, such as what distinguishes a Van Gogh from another. Importantly, the result will differ from the original dataset yet remain comparable.

d) Generative Adversarial Networks (GANs)

Imagine two players in a game: a generator and a discriminator.

    i. **Generator:** Consider a discriminator and a generator as two participants in a game.
    ii. **Discriminator:** Based on a dataset, the generator creates fresh data points and fake images.

In order to "fool" the detector, the designer becomes more skilled at producing realistic visuals. GANs generate high-quality images and videos by means of this adversarial training process: material produced by AI that could seem authentic.

e) Diffusion Models

As with a lump of clay being progressively shaped into a sculpture, these models begin with random noise and transform it into useful data. They gradually improve the data until it produces a result that is understandable and cohesive. Diffusion models are gaining traction as a competitive alternative to GANs because to their remarkable ability in producing high-resolution images.

f) Reinforcement Learning

Consider training a dog by rewarding excellent conduct with treats. In a similar vein, AI models are trained to make better judgements over time by learning the optimal course of action via incentives or penalties. In this manner, AI specialists and engineers may mould the intended functionality of AI models, optimising them to accomplish more precise objectives. For instance, while training models, AI engineers may utilise reinforcement learning to reward models that follow ethical standards.

g) Quantum Computing

Quantum computers are very powerful devices that can execute intricate calculations at a rate that surpasses that of conventional computers.

Quantum computing, which is still in its infancy, has the potential to significantly expand the capabilities of generative AI by managing larger datasets and more complex models more effectively. This could lead to significant improvements in processing power, pushing the limits of generative AI's capability while also reducing environmental costs.

1.2   Evolution of AI Techniques

Artificial Intelligence has experienced considerable development over time, moving through different methods that have transformed the way technology is engaged with and employed.

1.   Traditional Search

Traditional search methods are the cornerstone of information retrieval. Using these methods, users enter queries into search engines, which comb through enormous databases to provide pertinent results. This method is effective for rapidly obtaining a large amount of information since it mainly uses indexing and retrieval algorithms.

a) **Significance:** The capacity of traditional search to provide quick access to large volumes of data makes it essential. It is accessible to a wide range of users because to its ease of use and low interaction requirements.

b) **When to Use:** For typical information retrieval tasks, where the objective is to swiftly locate relevant material from huge datasets, traditional search is perfect. It is especially helpful for database enquiries, online searches, and other scenarios where consumers require fast responses to certain queries.

2. Prompt Engineering

A major advancement in AI interaction is prompt engineering, in which users create customised prompts to get the answers they want from AI models. This method uses large language models (LLMs) such as GPT to produce writing that is human-like in response to input prompts.

a) **Significance:** Rapid prototyping and adaptation are made possible by prompt engineering. By continually improving prompts, it allows users to customise replies, which makes it very flexible and effective for producing personalised information.

b) **When to Use:** Prompt Engineering is perfect for creative projects, content creation, and situations requiring precise, nuanced answers. Additionally, it is helpful in applications such as personalised communication, marketing content production, and customer assistance.

3. Retrieval-Augmented Generation (RAG)

The advantages of generative models and conventional search are combined in RAG. In order to provide precise and contextually relevant answers, it extracts pertinent data from a corpus.

a) **Significance:** By using external or real-time data, RAG improves the created content's relevancy and correctness. This makes it useful for applications that need accurate facts and current information.

b) **When to Use:** RAG works well for projects that need to integrate real data and have generating capabilities. Examples include chatbots, question-answering systems, and any other application where contextual correctness is crucial.

4. Fine-tuning

In order to customise an AI model's answers to specific tasks, fine-tuning entails training the model on a particular dataset. This method improves the model's capacity to provide precise and specialised outputs.

a) **Significance:** Fine-tuning is essential for activities requiring accuracy and domain-specific knowledge since it provides high specialisation and customised responses.

b) **When to Use:** Applications where pre-trained models' general skills need to be modified for particular tasks are the ideal candidates for fine-tuning. This covers domains such as legal document analysis, medical diagnostics, and any specific industrial applications.

5. Agentic AI

The pinnacle of AI evolution is represented by agentic AI, which enables models to execute tasks and make decisions automatically. These AI bots use large datasets and complex algorithms to function independently.

a) **Significance:** Agentic AI turns AI from a task-assistance tool into an independent agent capable of carrying out intricate tasks without the need for human assistance. This has significant effects on scalability, efficiency, and automation.

b) **When to Use:** When autonomous decision-making is needed in complex and dynamic situations, agentic AI is perfect. This covers fields including financial trading, robots, driverless cars, and smart home automation.

1.3   Applications of Generative Models

A generative model produces abstractions or representations of observable events or target variables using statistical and probabilistic techniques together with artificial intelligence (AI). It is therefore possible to create new data that resembles the observed data using these representations.

In order to represent events in data and help computers comprehend the actual world, generative modelling is employed in unsupervised machine learning (ML). Modelled data can be utilised to forecast a wide range of probability about a subject using this AI knowledge. A subclass of statistical models known as generative models creates new instances of data.

Applications for generative models are many and span many different domains. Below is a summary of some of the most important areas:

1.   **Image generation:**

The generative adversarial networks (GANs) are often used to produce photorealistic pictures that may be employed in a variety of fields, such as video game development, interior design, and fashion. For example, they may create lifelike human faces or other commercial components.

2. Art creation:

Generative models are increasingly being used by musicians and artists to produce fresh and avant-garde works of art. The art industry has seen a transformation because to tools like Midjourney, which allow artists to create beautiful images in response to text prompts or certain art styles.

3. Drug discovery:

Drug development is being expedited by generative AI models, which create novel chemical structures, forecast their characteristics, and optimise them for qualities like safety and effectiveness. This method improves the accuracy of finding viable drug candidates while saving time and money by assisting researchers in exploring a larger chemical space.

4. Content creation:

Website owners are increasingly employing generative models using tools like Copy.ai and HubSpot AI Content Writer to expedite their content production process. For instance, these artificial intelligence (AI) technologies may produce blog articles, social media content, email marketing content, and landing page text by given prompts or subjects. Generative models facilitate the

production of material more quickly while preserving
consistency and quality. To guarantee accuracy, relevance,
and a distinctive brand voice, human monitoring is always
required when producing content.

5. Video games:

By automating a variety of activities, including the creation
of realistic textures, three-dimensional models, and
animations, generative models speed up the production of
video games. The models provide dynamic, intelligent
non-player characters (NPCs) with a variety of game
settings and levels. Generative models allow developers to
concentrate on core gameplay by automating tedious tasks
and producing imaginative material, which leads to more
inventive and engrossing gaming experiences.

6. Image-to-image translation:

Using deep learning approaches, generative models learn
to map several picture representations together to give
image-to-image translation. For example, models like
GANs may turn crude drawings into realistic pictures or a
greyscale image into a coloured one.

7. Text-to-image translation:

Textual descriptions may be translated into related visuals
using generative models, which has uses in content
production and advertising. Concepts stated in words are
visualised via text-to-image technology.

8. Video generation:

Generative models, like GANs, use preexisting video data to identify patterns and produce synthetic video content. They create new sequences that imitate the original style by analysing frame connections, motion, and visual components. Applications like virtual reality, entertainment, and advertising where dynamic, captivating material is essential are supported by this capacity.

9. Audio generation:

Generative models have made tremendous progress in the creation of music and speech synthesis. For example, deep learning methods are used by models like WaveNet and Tacotron to produce very expressive and natural-sounding synthetic speech, which finds usage in voice-overs, audiobooks, and virtual assistants. In the music industry, models like Jukedeck and Musenet utilise machine-learning algorithms to create unique music by examining large datasets of previously recorded songs. Background soundtracks for a variety of multimedia projects are provided by this technology, which also helps musicians in their art.

1.4   Ethics in Generative AI

Generative AI tools can provide assistance in daily life, in the workplace, or during study sessions. As with any instrument, its usage must be appropriate, evaluative, and ethical. The following outlines ethical considerations related to generative AI for exploration.

1. Environmental Impacts

The process of constructing, training, and utilising generative AI models demands a considerable amount of energy and results in carbon emissions. A significant amount of water is also used for cooling purposes. Researchers and companies are investigating methods to enhance the sustainability of generative AI. However, it remains crucial to evaluate whether the application of AI justifies its environmental consequences and to utilise generative AI tools as efficiently as possible.

2. Accessibility

While numerous generative AI tools remain available at no charge, an increasing number are introducing fees for access or for utilising premium features. This establishes obstacles for individuals who cannot afford access. Nonetheless, generative AI tools may serve as aids for accessibility. For instance, Maggie Melo discussed ChatGPT as a helpful tool for teachers and students with Attention-Deficit/Hyperactivity Disorder (ADHD).

3. Creatorship and Academic Integrity

University experiences enhance knowledge and skills, ensuring that upon completing a degree, individuals are well-prepared for employment or additional studies. Employing generative AI to produce content without further elaboration, alteration, or significant interaction results in the presentation of work that does not belong to the individual, and it indicates a lack of personal knowledge and skill development.

Utilising a generative AI tool to produce or modify an assignment and subsequently presenting that work as original is considered dishonest. This resembles requesting another individual to perform tasks on behalf of oneself. When utilising generative AI, it is essential to disclose the specific tool(s) employed and the manner in which they were used. Additionally, if there is an intention to publish work that includes content generated by AI, it is advisable to review the publisher's guidelines regarding what is permissible.

4. Copyright

Numerous copyright concerns are associated with the creation and application of generative AI tools. The gathering of training data for the AI tool, the inclusion of copyright-protected material, and the necessity of obtaining permission or a license from the rights holder are all significant factors to consider. The utilisation of significant segments of works protected by copyright as inputs or specific forms of outputs with AI tools could carry copyright consequences.

Although there does not yet seem to be a legal foundation for copyright protection of AI-generated outputs in various nations, these outputs may violate other copyrights, and both generative AI tool developers and users may be held liable for such infringements.

5. Rights Management

The emergence of generative AI introduces intricate difficulties regarding rights management. The rapid advancement of technology necessitates that regulatory activities take time to adapt and mirror these developments. An example of this issue involves artists and writers whose content has been utilised to train generative AI.

The implications of content contributions represent a crucial aspect of rights management that individuals should understand prior to utilising generative AI tools. Submitting content to AI platforms via prompts or uploads may grant an AI tool the right to reuse and distribute that content, potentially leading to a violation of copyright or privacy. Caution is advised when submitting content, particularly information or data that was not originally created by the individual, to AI platforms.

6. Privacy And Data Security

Generative models that utilise personal data present privacy concerns, as they have the potential to create synthetic profiles that bear a strong resemblance to actual individuals. This may result in infringements of user privacy and legal repercussions, including breaches of data protection laws such as General Data Protection Regulation (GDPR).

Data anonymisation during training and the implementation of strong data security measures, including encryption, are crucial for protecting user data. The danger of privacy breaches may also be reduced by following guidelines like the GDPR's data minimisation requirements.

7. Bias And Discrimination

Generative models have the potential to perpetuate biases that exist in the datasets used for training, resulting in unjust discrimination. Biassed facial recognition software has the potential to misidentify individuals, leading to legal complications and harm to reputations.

A recent instance involves Google's Gemini, which encountered backlash after users found that it was generating images that were historically inaccurate. These included images of a female Pope, Black Vikings, and an Asian lady dressed in a German soldier outfit from World War II.

To address this issue, prioritising diversity in training datasets is essential. Additionally, it is important to perform regular audits to detect and correct any unintended biases. Collaborating with organisations that focus on bias assessments and audits can enhance the fairness of generative AI systems.

8. Accuracy

It is common for companies to withhold information regarding the data utilised for training a generative AI model. Generative AI is unable to inform a user about the data utilised to create specific content, nor can it provide accurate citations or generate a dependable bibliography. As a result, material produced by generative AI lacks credibility and reliability as a source of information.

AI models can occasionally generate inaccurate, biassed, or obsolete information. In certain instances, a generative AI tool may indicate that it cannot deliver an accurate response, while in other situations, it might produce an incorrect answer that seems to be valid. This phenomenon is referred to as a "hallucination." For instance, ChatGPT sometimes creates fake citations to unidentified sources. To prevent the use or dissemination of false information, it is essential to confirm the correctness of content produced by AI through trustworthy sources prior to incorporating it into any work.

1.5   What Is Discriminative AI?

The goal of discriminative AI is to learn from training data and how sample data distinguishes between different classes in order to choose the best option or the appropriate class for the input data. Since discriminative AI models are taught to distinguish between various types of data, they perform better than generative AI models in this regard.

These models aim to discover the connection between labels or categorical variables and their inputs. Natural language processing, image and speech recognition, and predictive analytics across a variety of platforms and applications using methods like logistic regression and support vector machines (SVM) are some of the most common use cases for AI models.

1. **Features of Discriminative AI**

These are the main features of discriminative AI:

a. **Classification Accuracy:** Performs better than others in terms of accuracy and efficiency when it comes to classifying data into predefined categories.

b. **Pattern Recognition:** The input data set's structures and features are described and differentiated.

c. **Predictive Power:** Predictive power can use learnt models in training to forecast the features of future incoming unknown data sets.

d. **Efficiency:** Training models can occasionally be more efficient than generative models.

e. **Application Versatility:** In cutting-edge domains like sentiment analysis, fraud detection, diagnostics, and spam filtering, it is prevalent.

2. **Uses of Discriminative AI**

In many different sectors, discriminative AI is essential for pattern detection and classification:

a. **Image Recognition:** Distinguishing between various species in wildlife photography, for example, occurs through the identification of objects in photographs.

b. **Speech Recognition:** The process of converting spoken language into text involves the classification of sound patterns.

c. **Natural Language Processing (NLP):** Utilised in the development of chatbot responses, sentiment analysis, and spam detection.

d. **Healthcare:** The classification of medical images or laboratory results to aid in the diagnosis of diseases.

e. **Finance:** Making the distinction between authentic and fraudulent transactions improves fraud detection.

f. **Retail & Marketing:** Enhancing personalised recommendations by examining consumer preferences.

In applications like picture and voice recognition, it is essential to correctly categorise each data point since a single incorrect classification might result in large inaccuracies in the model's predictions.

3. Working of Discriminative AI

Discriminative AI models are trained on labelled datasets using supervised learning, which enables them to identify unique patterns and decision boundaries in the input data. The procedure entails:

a. **Training on Labelled Data:** Labelled training data, such as pictures with the labels "cat" or "dog," are input into the model.

b. **Feature Extraction:** It picks up essential characteristics that set classes apart, including fur texture or shape.

c. **Decision Boundary Formation:** The model establishes borders according to learnt characteristics to divide various classes.

d. **Classification of New Data:** The model uses the patterns it has learnt to accurately identify input based on the recognised data points when it is presented with unknown data.

The following are well-known machine learning techniques for discriminative AI:

- Logistic regression is used for applications involving binary classification.
- SVMs (support vector machines) are used to draw borders around decisions.
- Neural networks, such as CNNs and RNNs, are used in deep learning applications such as voice and picture recognition.

4. The Future of Discriminative AI

Discriminative models are become more accurate and effective as AI technology develops, combining with deep learning to achieve even more precision. They are being used more and more in real-time applications where precise categorisation is essential, such cybersecurity, driverless cars, and medical diagnostics.

Future discriminatory AI models will be more open, equitable, and interpretable thanks to continuous advancements in AI ethics and bias reduction, guaranteeing ethical AI development across a range of businesses. Further improving the comprehension and effectiveness of machine learning algorithms, these models will be essential in modelling data points for next applications.

1.6   AI in a Nutshell

The goal of the computer science discipline known as artificial intelligence (AI) is to make computers, computer-controlled robots, and software that behave intelligently like the human mind. In order to develop intelligent software and systems, the fundamental idea of artificial intelligence is to investigate the patterns and mechanisms of human cognition.

AI studies the human brain in great detail in an effort to comprehend how people see, learn, and make choices. AI researchers may create models and algorithms that mimic intelligent reasoning and problem-solving by identifying these cognitive processes.

AI's ultimate objective is to create machines that are capable of reasoning, experience-based learning, situational adaptation, and activities that normally call for human intellect.

1.   A brief History of Artificial Intelligence

The history of artificial intelligence (AI) is lengthy and includes several decades. An outline of significant turning points and advancements in the field is provided below:

a) **1950s:** The 1950s marked the beginning of the AI revolution, as researchers began to investigate the potential of machines to demonstrate intelligent behaviour. Prominent individuals like as Alan Turing introduced the concept of machine intelligence and created the well-known "Turing Test" to evaluate a computer's capacity for human-like intelligence.

b) **1956:** John McCarthy is credited for coining the phrase "artificial intelligence" and organising the Dartmouth Conference, which is regarded as the formal beginning of AI as a subject of study. Prominent scientists gathered at the meeting to discuss the potential and prospects of artificial intelligence.

c) **1960s-1970s:** Expert systems, or computer programs created to replicate the decision-making skills of human specialists in certain fields, were the major focus of AI research at this time. However, the intricacy of real-world issues and technological limits hindered the development of early AI systems.

d) **1980s-1990s:** AI went through "AI winter" during which funding and public attention declined. Research on AI slowed down, and the technology did not live up to expectations. Nonetheless, research in fields like natural language processing, knowledge representation, and machine learning persisted, laying the groundwork for further developments.

e) **Late 1990s-early 2000s:** AI had a comeback when processing power rose and new methods like data-driven approaches and neural networks became popular. Applications such as data mining, computer vision, and voice recognition began to indicate encouraging outcomes.

f) **2010s:** Due to developments in big data and deep learning, the 2010s saw important advances in artificial intelligence. Deep learning models, which are driven by multi-layered neural networks, have shown impressive results in a variety of tasks, including natural language processing, picture identification, and gaming.

g) **Present day:** These days, artificial intelligence (AI) permeates every aspect of life, from recommendation engines and virtual assistants to self-driving cars and medical diagnostics. As deep learning, reinforcement learning, and machine learning methods advance, they push the limits of artificial intelligence.

2. Weak AI vs. Strong AI

Weak AI and strong AI differ from one another in terms of their capacities and degree of human-like intelligence:

a) **Weak AI:** Weak AI systems are those that are designed to carry out certain activities or functions inside a restricted area. They are sometimes referred to as narrow AI or applied AI. Weak AI lacks universal intelligence and is only concerned with addressing particular challenges. These systems have been taught or designed to be very good at certain tasks, including chess play, picture classification, or voice recognition. They are unable to expand their knowledge or abilities outside of their designated area and work within well-defined parameters.

b) **Strong AI:** Strong AI, often known as Human-Level AI or Artificial General intellect (AGI), seeks to mimic human-level intellect in a variety of activities and areas. Robust artificial intelligence systems are able to comprehend, learn, and use information in ways that mimic human cognitive capacities. Similar to human intelligence, they are capable of consciousness, self-awareness, and reasoning. Strong AI aims to replicate the intricacy and flexibility of the human mind, allowing robots to demonstrate a broad range of cognitive abilities and carry out activities in a variety of fields.

3. **Applications of Artificial Intelligence**

There are several uses for artificial intelligence (AI) in a variety of sectors and businesses. Here are a few noteworthy applications of AI:

a) **Healthcare:** AI is transforming healthcare by helping with medication development, illness detection, and individualised therapy regimens. It makes it possible to analyse medical pictures for precise diagnosis, including MRIs and X-rays. AI-powered solutions may also help detect possible health hazards, forecast the course of diseases, and monitor patient data in real-time.

b) **Finance and Banking:** In the financial industry, AI is used in algorithmic trading, risk assessment, fraud detection, and customer support. Customer interactions are improved by AI-powered chatbots and virtual assistants, while machine learning algorithms examine financial data to identify trends and stop fraud.

c) **Transportation:** Autonomous cars, better traffic control systems, and route optimisation are all made possible by AI. AI algorithms are used by self-driving vehicles to navigate and make decisions, improving efficiency and safety. AI is also used in supply chain management and logistics to streamline processes and save expenses.

d) **E-commerce and Retail:** Demand forecasts, consumer behaviour research, and tailored product suggestions all make use of AI. Chatbots with AI capabilities help consumers locate items and provide assistance. Visual search and item identification are made possible by computer vision technology, which improves shopping online.

e) **Manufacturing and Robotics:** Automation and robots powered by AI improve industrial processes by increasing productivity, accuracy, and efficiency. Artificial intelligence-enabled robots are capable of handling quality control, performing difficult tasks, and working in hazardous settings.

f) **Smart Homes and Internet of Things (IoT):** Automated illumination, security systems, smart thermostats, and voice-controlled assistants are all made possible by AI, which improves the functionality of smart home devices. IoT data is analysed by AI algorithms to enhance home automation and optimise energy use.

g) **Customer Service:** In customer service, chatbots and virtual assistants driven by AI are being used more and more to answer questions, give real-time assistance, and manage repetitive duties. Natural language comprehension, interaction learning, and individualised support are all capabilities of these AI systems.

These are just a few of the many industries that are using AI, including cybersecurity, education, agriculture, and entertainment. AI's adaptability enables it to revolutionise a range of sectors, optimise workflows, and provide creative answers to challenging issues.

4. Examples of Artificial Intelligence

Many facets of our everyday lives have been impacted by artificial intelligence (AI), which is transforming industries and improving user experiences. The following

noteworthy instances highlight the variety of AI
applications:

a) **ChatGPT:** ChatGPT, an advanced language model
from OpenAI, is useful for chatbots, virtual
assistants, and customer care since it can have
natural language conversations. Deep learning
methods are used to produce answers that are
human-like.

b) **Google Maps:** Google Maps provides traffic
updates, real-time navigation, and tailored
suggestions by using AI algorithms. In order to
recommend the best routes and forecast
congestion, it examines a large amount of data,
including past traffic trends and user input.

c) **Smart Assistants:** AI-powered smart assistants that
can comprehend voice requests, deliver
information, and carry out activities include Google
Assistant, Apple's Siri, and Amazon's Alexa. These
assistants can comprehend human intent and
provide pertinent replies thanks to machine
learning and natural language processing.

d) **Tesla Autopilot:** Semi-autonomous driving is
made possible in Tesla automobiles via the
Autopilot system, which makes use of AI and
sophisticated sensors. It can help with adaptive
cruise control, lane changes, and steering.

e) **Google Translate and DeepL:** These products
provide real-time multilingual language translation

services by using artificial intelligence technology such as machine learning and neural networks.

f) **Netflix Recommendation System:** Netflix analyses customer preferences and watching patterns using AI algorithms to provide tailored movie and TV program suggestions.

g) **IBM Watson for Oncology:** Healthcare professionals use IBM Watson's AI capabilities to help oncologists make decisions about cancer treatments. It provides personalised treatment suggestions by analysing medical literature and patient data.

h) **DeepMind's AlphaGo:** An artificial intelligence software called AlphaGo, created by DeepMind, a Google company, demonstrated impressive performance in the board game Go. It demonstrated the potential of AI in challenging strategic games by defeating world Go champion Lee Sedol.

i) **Sophia the Robot:** A humanoid robot with AI skills and a human-like appearance, Sophia was created by Hanson Robotics. It advances social robots by displaying emotions, recognising faces, and having conversations.

CHAPTER 2: FUNDAMENTALS OF MACHINE LEARNING

Learning Objective

This chapter covers the basics of Machine Learning, its different types, algorithms, and data preprocessing techniques. It also discusses model evaluation strategies, providing a strong foundation for understanding how ML powers Generative AI.

2.1   What Is Machine Learning?

Machine learning is a subfield of artificial intelligence that allows algorithms to identify concealed patterns in datasets. They are able to forecast fresh, comparable data without the need for explicit task programming. Applications for machine learning may be found in many different domains, including fraud detection, portfolio optimisation, recommendation systems, natural language processing, picture and audio recognition, and automation of tasks.

The influence of machine learning extends to robotics, drones, and driverless cars, improving their capacity to adapt to changing conditions. This method, which is tightly related to data mining and data science, is a breakthrough in which computers learn from data examples to provide correct results.

1. Need for Machine Learning

The significance of machine learning lies in its capacity to enable computers to enhance their performance on specific tasks by learning from data without the need for explicit programming. Machine learning is especially helpful for activities involving a lot of data, complicated decision-making, and dynamic contexts because of its capacity to learn from data and adapt to new circumstances.

The following are some particular domains in which machine learning finds application:

a) **Predictive Modelling:** Businesses may improve their decision-making by using machine learning to create predictive models. For instance, machine learning can be employed to forecast which consumers are most likely to purchase a specific product or which patients are most susceptible to developing a specific disease.

b) **Natural Language Processing:** To create systems that can comprehend and interpret human language, machine learning is used. For applications like chatbots, speech recognition, and language translation, this is crucial.

c) **Computer Vision:** Systems that are able to identify and comprehend photos and videos are created using machine learning. This is critical for applications like medical imaging, surveillance systems, and self-driving automobiles.

d) **Fraud Detection:** Detecting fraudulent activity in internet advertising, financial transactions, and other domains is possible using machine learning.

e) **Recommendation Systems:** Recommendation systems that provide recommendations to users based on their prior behaviour and preferences may be developed using machine learning.

Overall, machine learning has emerged as a crucial tool for several companies and sectors, allowing them to harness data more effectively, enhance their decision-making procedures, and provide more personalised consumer experiences.

2. Working of Machine Learning Algorithms

Machine learning algorithms are not explicitly coded for every task instead, they learn patterns and correlations from data to produce predictions or choices. This is a condensed description of the workings of a common machine learning algorithm:

a) Data Collection

First, pertinent information is gathered or vetted. This information may consist of text, photos, numerical data, or other characteristics, traits, or examples that are relevant to the work at hand.

b) Data Preprocessing

It is often necessary to preprocess the data before entering it into the algorithm. This stage might include separating the data into training and test sets, cleaning the data (dealing with missing values, outliers), and converting the data (normalisation, scaling).

c) Choosing a Model

A machine learning model that is appropriate for the task is selected based on the classification, regression, and clustering tasks. Some examples are decision trees, neural networks, support vector machines, and more complex models like deep learning frameworks.

d) Training the Model

The training data is used to train the chosen model. The program discovers links and patterns in the data during training. This entails repeatedly modifying the model's parameters to reduce the discrepancy between the training data's actual outputs (labels or targets) and projected outputs.

e) Evaluating the Model

After training, the model's performance is assessed using the test data. Measures like mean squared error, recall, accuracy, and precision are used to assess how effectively the model generalises to new, untested data.

f) Fine-tuning

In order to enhance performance, models may be adjusted by modifying hyperparameters, which are factors that are not directly learnt during training, such as learning rate or the number of hidden layers in a neural network.

g) Prediction or Inference

Lastly, fresh data is subjected to predictions or judgements based on the trained model. In this procedure, the learnt patterns are applied to fresh inputs to produce outputs, such as numerical values for regression tasks or class labels for classification tasks.

3. Machine Learning Lifecycle

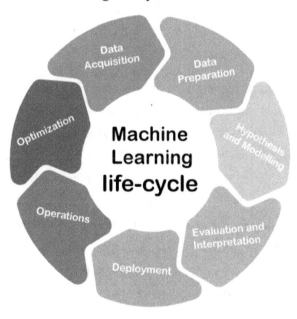

Figure 2.1: Machine Learning Life Cycle. [1]

The major steps involved in the machine learning life cycle are outlined as follows:

---

[1]https://miro.medium.com/v2/resize:fit:640/format:webp/0*riH9z
2sLjb4eAQcf.png

a) Data Acquisition

Data serves as a crucial element in the life cycle of machine learning, yet it is necessary to obtain suitable data to address a specific problem. No data scientist is needed to collect the data. A person with prior knowledge of the actual differences among the various freely available data sets, along with the ability to make impactful decisions regarding an organisation's investment strategy, would be most suitable for the role of a data scientist.

b) Data Preparation

This task could be considered the most laborious and time-intensive in this cycle, as it requires the identification of numerous data quality issues. Typically, when data is obtained, it cannot be analysed due to the presence of incorrect entries, inconsistencies, and semantic mistakes. To utilise this type of data, data scientists manually reformat and clean it by either editing it in a spreadsheet or by scripting code. The data wrangling phase or data cleansing step are additional names for the data preparation process.

c) Hypothesis and Modelling

This is the basic phase of any data science project, which involves creating, executing, and improving the programs in order to analyse the data and extract valuable business insights. Programs can be developed using languages such as Python, R, MATLAB, or Perl. At this stage, the data is

utilised to train different machine learning algorithms, and
the algorithm that yields the best performance is chosen.

d) Evaluation and Interpretation

After the training of the model on data, the final outcome
is assessed to determine its performance and reliability in
practical scenarios. Every performance metric possesses a
unique set of evaluation metrics. For example, when
aiming for a machine learning model to forecast daily
stock, it is strongly advised to take into account the RMSE
(root mean squared error) for assessment purposes.
Alternatively, performance metrics such as average
accuracy, AUC, and log loss are taken into account for the
classification of spam emails.

e) Deployment

Deployment refers to the application of a model that
utilises new data to generate predictions. Creating a model
is typically not the conclusion of the project. Although the
model aims to enhance the understanding of the data, the
acquired insights must be structured and displayed in a
manner that allows for easy utilisation by the client. The
deployment phase can range from being as
straightforward as generating a report to being as complex
as implementing a replicable data science process based on
specific requirements.

f) Operations

A plan is created for overseeing and maintaining the data
science project over an extended period. In this phase, the

performance of the model is monitored regarding its upgrades and downgrades. Data scientists utilise a specific data science project to facilitate shared learning and enhance the execution of similar data science projects in the future.

g) Optimisation

The last stage of every data science endeavour is optimisation. When fresh data sources are added or when essential actions are taken to improve the machine learning model's performance, it retrains the model in production.

2.2   Types of Machine Learning

Numerous types of machine learning techniques exist, each possessing unique characteristics and applications. Several common types of machine learning algorithms utilised in daily life include the following:

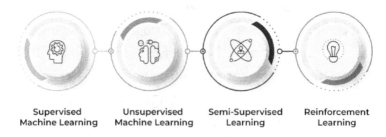

| Supervised Machine Learning | Unsupervised Machine Learning | Semi-Supervised Learning | Reinforcement Learning |

Figure 2.2: Types of Machine Learning. [2]

_____

[2]https://zd-brightspot.s3.us-east-1.amazonaws.com/wp-content/uploads/2022/04/04094802/4-12-1-e1715637495321.png

1. Supervised Learning

One of the most significant categories of machine learning
algorithms is supervised learning, in which the algorithm
is trained on labelled data. This indicates that input-output
pairs with known valid outputs are included in the data
supplied to the algorithm. The algorithm gains knowledge
from this data by identifying correlations and patterns
between the inputs and outputs. The model may use what
it has learnt to forecast the outcome for fresh, unknown
data once it has been trained.

a) Example of Supervised Learning

A situation arises in which there is a requirement to
develop a model for categorising various kinds of fruits.
The process begins with providing the algorithm a
collection of images depicting various fruits, with each
image tagged to indicate the specific type of fruit it shows,
including apples, bananas, and oranges. The algorithm
acquires the ability to identify the characteristics that set
different fruits apart, such as shape, colour, and size.
When a new image of a fruit that the algorithm has not
encountered before is inputted later, it will utilise the
learnt patterns to determine if the fruit is an apple, banana,
or orange. This process explains the functioning of
supervised learning.

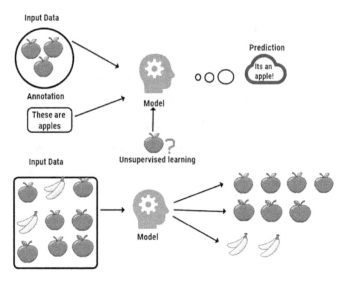

Figure 2.3: Supervised Learning. [3]

b) Types of Supervised Learning

The supervised learning algorithm can be divided into two primary categories: Classification Learning and Regression Learning.

i. Classification Learning

Sorting data into distinct classes or groups is the aim of classification learning, a kind of supervised learning. A labelled dataset, in which every data point is linked to a predetermined category, is used to train the algorithm. For instance, in an email spam filter, the algorithm becomes

---

[3]https://images.prismic.io/encord/f1fa13a6-88a3-4c20-b620-46489fe00f45_What+is+Supervised+Learning+%7C+Encord.png?
auto=compress,format

adept at categorising emails as either "spam" or "not spam" based on attributes such as the subject line, originator, and content.

The following are some typical classification learning algorithms:

- Logistic Regression
- Support Vector Machine
- Random Forest
- Decision Tree
- K-Nearest Neighbours (KNN)
- Naive Bayes.

ii. Regression Learning

The goal of regression learning, a different kind of supervised learning, is to forecast a continuous value as opposed to a category. A labelled dataset containing input-output pairs—where the output is a numerical value—is used to train the algorithm. For instance, the system learns from characteristics like location, number of bedrooms, and square foot area to anticipate home values. Using this data, the algorithm forecasts a new home's price depending on its attributes. Finding stock price projections, predicting economic patterns, and many more situations are just a few of the numerous applications for regression.

Typical algorithms used in regression learning methods include the following:

- Linear Regression
- Polynomial Regression
- Ridge Regression
- Lasso Regression
- Decision tree
- Random Forest.

2.   Unsupervised Learning

In unsupervised learning, an algorithm is given data without labels or predetermined categories, making it one of the most popular forms of machine learning techniques. Finding patterns or correlations in the data is the primary objective of this program. Rather than being instructed on what to search for, the algorithm automatically finds common traits and clusters related data pieces. This is helpful for identifying hidden patterns, putting related things in one category, or minimising the volume of data for further analysis.

a)   Example of Unsupervised Learning

A dataset is envisioned that includes different books along with their characteristics such as genre, author, page count, and year of publication. An unsupervised learning system may use clustering to combine related books according to these characteristics. This will unveil a collection of novels that are either authored by the same author or fall under certain categories. Bookshops have the ability to utilise this information for better inventory organisation or to suggest comparable books to their customers.

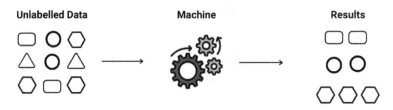

Figure 2.4: Unsupervised Machine Learning. [4]

b) Types of Unsupervised Learning

There are two primary categories of unsupervised learning, which are association and clustering.

i. Clustering in Unsupervised Learning

In unsupervised learning, clustering is a process where data points are grouped by algorithm based on similarities. Data points in each cluster, or group, are more comparable to one another than to individual data points in other clusters. Clustering is a technique used in many different domains, such as customer segmentation, where it allows firms to group clients with similar purchase behaviours and tailor distinct marketing campaigns for each customer.

---

[4]https://media.licdn.com/dms/image/v2/D5612AQEPphQDz-Lv5A/article-cover_image-shrink_720_1280/article-cover_image-shrink_720_1280/0/1712325585473?e=2147483647&v=beta&t=nSD XRawEFm4fWbKBD59-3IsDNwUCP0csrTi2w6sVxYA

The following are a few popular clustering algorithms:

- K-Means Clustering algorithm
- Mean-shift algorithm
- DBSCAN Algorithm
- Principal Component Analysis
- Independent Component Analysis.

ii.   Association in Unsupervised Learning

In unsupervised learning, association is a technique for finding intriguing correlations or trends across variables in large datasets. The rules that emphasise the relationship between the occurrence of one item and the occurrence of another are identified using this approach. For instance, an association algorithm may show that consumers who purchase bread are also likely to purchase butter in a market basket study. These association rules are used by businesses to enhance inventory control and product positioning.

The following are a few popular association rule learning algorithms:

- Apriori Algorithm
- Eclat
- FP-growth Algorithm

3.   Semi-Supervised Learning

Semi-supervised learning is another popular machine learning approach that makes use of a lot of unlabelled data and a small quantity of labelled data. While the labelled data helps in the model's learning to generate predictions, the unlabelled data enhances the model's accuracy by offering more details about the data's structure.

a)   Example of Semi-Supervised Learning

Consider the process of creating a model that categorises emails into spam and non-spam classifications. A collection of 100 labelled emails exists, categorised as either "spam" or "not spam," alongside 1000 unlabelled emails. In semi-supervised learning, the process begins with training the model using 100 labelled emails. After the model has been constructed, it is utilised to forecast labels for the 1000 emails that lack labels. The predictions are not always accurate, yet they offer supplementary information. This process aids the model in gaining a deeper understanding of the features and patterns present in the emails, leading to enhanced performance.

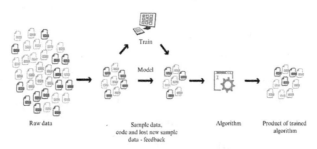

Figure 2.5: Semi-Supervised Learning. [5]

---

[5]https://www.researchgate.net/publication/357876249/figure/fig3/AS:1113122534375425@1642400501759/Working-model-of-semi-supervised-learning-10.png

b) Types of Semi-Supervised Learning

Numerous semi-supervised learning models exist, each with distinct characteristics and employed for distinct objectives.

i. **Graph-based Semi-Supervised Learning:** The connections between data points are represented by graphs in these models. Through these links, labels are dispersed from marked to unlabelled places.

ii. **Label Propagation:** Using this paradigm, labels are transferred from labelled to unlabelled data via a network, supposing that comparable data points are near one another.

iii. **Co-training:** This method labels the unlabelled data by training two or more distinct models. Different portions of the data are utilised to train each model, and the predictions made by each model are used to enhance the others.

iv. **Self-training:** After training the labelled data, the model makes predictions about the unlabelled data. The model is retrained when these fresh predictions are included in the training set.

4. Reinforcement Learning

Reinforcement learning is a form of machine learning in which an agent acquires the ability to make decisions by executing actions in an environment in order to attain the highest possible reward. The agent learns via trial and error, starting with no prior knowledge of the optimal course of action. Every action has an outcome, which may be either a reward or a punishment. The agent seeks to choose behaviours that provide the maximum cumulative reward throughout the given time period.

a) Example of Reinforcement Learning

Consider the process of teaching a dog to catch a ball. The setting is the yard, the participant is the dog, and the activity involves retrieving the ball. When the dog retrieves the ball, a treat is given as a reward. If the dog fails to retrieve the ball or engages in another activity, it does not earn a treat, which serves as a negative reward.

At the beginning, the dog might not grasp the task, but with time, it comes to realise that retrieving the ball results in a reward. The dog's objective is to obtain additional rewards by retrieving more balls. The dog's fetching habit increases with repeated encounters and incentives.

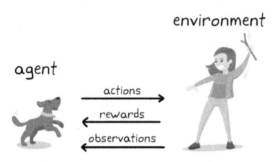

Figure 2.6: Reinforcement learning. [6]

---

[6]https://www.mathworks.com/discovery/reinforcement-learning/_jcr_content/mainParsys3/discoverysubsection_6030982

b) Types of Reinforcement Learning

There are three primary varieties of reinforcement learning techniques, each of which is employed for a distinct purpose and possesses distinct characteristics.

i. Q-learning

Q-learning is a straightforward and well-liked reinforcement learning method. It stores values that indicate the anticipated future benefits of doing a certain action in a particular condition using a Q-table. In order to maximise its total reward, the agent gradually learns the best course of action in each state and adjusts the Q-values in response to the rewards it receives.

ii. SARSA (State-Action-Reward-State-Action)

Similar to Q-learning, SARSA is another reinforcement learning method; however, instead of updating the Q-values according to the optimal course of action, it bases them on the action the agent actually does. This guarantees that the agent learns in accordance with the existing policy and makes SARSA more conservative.

2.3   Machine Learning Algorithms

The AI system's mode of operation, which often involves predicting output values from input data, is called a machine learning algorithm. Regression and classification

16/mainParsys3/image.adapt.full.medium.png/1724847000082.png

are the two primary steps in machine learning (ML) algorithms.

In essence, machine learning algorithms are collections of instructions that, without explicit programming, enable computers to learn from data, generate predictions, and gradually improve their performance. Three major categories can be used to classify machine learning algorithms:

a. **Supervised Learning:** Labelled data, in which the link between input and outcome is understood, is what algorithms learn from.

b. **Unsupervised Learning:** Algorithms find patterns or groups in unlabelled data.

c. **Reinforcement Learning:** Algorithms acquire knowledge through interaction with an environment and feedback in the form of rewards or penalties.

1. Supervised Learning Algorithms

Supervised learning algorithms are trained on datasets in which each example is associated with a target or response variable, which is referred to as the label. To enable the model to provide precise predictions on unseen data, the objective is to develop a mapping function from input data to the associated output labels.

The two primary categories of supervised learning algorithms are classification and regression.

a. **Classification:** Classification properly assigns test results into distinct groups using an algorithm. The system identifies certain entities in the dataset and makes an effort to determine how those things need to be described or labelled. Random forests, K-nearest neighbour, decision trees, support vector machines (SVM), and linear classifiers are examples of common classification algorithms.

b. **Regression:** Regression is employed to comprehend the correlation between independent and dependent variables. It is often used to forecast things like a company's sales revenue. Popular regression methods include polynomial, logistic, and linear regression.

Supervised machine learning processes use a variety of calculation methods and algorithms, which are often computed using Python and other similar programs. Among the supervised learning algorithms are:

a. **AdaBoost or gradient boosting:** Adaptive boosting is another name for this strategy, which combines a regression algorithm that performs poorly with weaker ones to make it stronger and produce less errors. The predicting ability of many base estimators is combined in boosting.

b. **Artificial neural networks:** Also referred to as ANNs, neural networks, or simulated neural networks (SNNs), they are a subset of machine learning techniques that are the foundation of deep

learning algorithms. The learner algorithm uses
building blocks called neurones, which are
modelled after the trained and adjusted neurones
in the human brain, to identify patterns in
incoming data.

c. **Decision tree algorithms**: Decision trees, which
may be shown with a tree diagram, use a branching
series of connected choices to categorise data into
categories and forecast numerical values
(regression issues). In contrast to the neural
network's dark box, decision trees have the benefit
of being simple to verify and audit.

d. **Dimensionality reduction**: A chosen data
collection is said to have high dimensionality if it
contains a large number of features. The most
significant ideas or information are then left behind
after dimensionality reduction reduces the number
of characteristics. An illustration is principal
component analysis.

e. **K-nearest neighbour**: This non-parametric
technique, sometimes referred to as KNN, groups
data points according to their associations and
closeness to other accessible data. It makes the
assumption that comparable data points may be
located close to one another. Therefore, it aims to
determine the distance between data points, often
using the Euclidean distance, and then classifies the
data according to the average or most common
category.

f. **Linear regression**: Linear regression is employed to establish a correlation between a dependent variable and one or more independent variables, usually in order to make predictions about future outcomes. Simple linear regression is the process of analysing data with just one independent variable and one dependent variable.

g. **Logistic regression**: Logistic regression is used when the dependent variable is categorical, meaning that there are binary outputs, such as "true" and "false" or "yes" and "no," while linear regression is used when the dependent variables are continuous. Logistic regression is primarily employed to address binary classification issues, including spam detection, even though both regression models aim to comprehend the connections between data inputs.

h. **Neural networks**: Neural networks, which are mostly used for deep learning algorithms, use layers of nodes to analyse incoming training data in a manner that replicates the interconnectedness of the human brain. Inputs, weights, a bias (threshold), and an output comprise each node. Data is transmitted to the subsequent stratum in the network when the output value surpasses a specified threshold, causing the node to "fire" or activate. Neural networks use gradient descent to learn from modifications depending on the loss function. The accuracy of the model may be trusted when the cost function is at or close to zero.

i. **Naïve Bayes**: This method uses the Bayes Theorem's class conditional independence principle. This indicates that each predictor has an equal influence on a particular outcome and that the existence of one characteristic does not affect the presence of another in the likelihood of that event. Multinomial Naïve Bayes, Bernoulli Naïve Bayes, and Gaussian Naïve Bayes are the three varieties of Naïve Bayes classifiers. Text categorisation, spam detection, and recommendation systems are the main applications for this technology.

j. **Random forests**: A random forest is a machine learning approach that combines the output of many decision trees to predict a value or category. Uncorrelated decision trees are referred to as the "forest" because they are put together to lower variance and provide forecasts that are more accurate.

k. **Support vector machines (SVM)**: Usually, this approach creates a hyperplane when the distance between two classes of data points is at its highest. It may be used to both regression and data classification issues. The classifications of data points (oranges vs. apples) on each side of the hyperplane are separated by what is called the decision boundary.

2. Unsupervised Learning Algorithms

Unsupervised learning algorithms use unlabelled data to find underlying structures or patterns without producing predetermined results. Based on their intended use, they are again separated into three primary groups: Dimensionality Reduction, Association Rule Mining, and Clustering.

a) Clustering

Clustering algorithms use similarities or differences to organise data points into clusters. Finding organic groups in the data is the aim. Various kinds of clustering algorithms may be distinguished by the ways in which they group data. Among these categories are "density-based methods, connectivity-based methods, distribution-based methods, and centroid-based methods."

i. **Centroid-based Methods:** Utilise central elements, such as centroids or medoids, to represent concentrations.
   - **K-Means clustering:** Assuming spherical clusters, iteratively assigns points to the closest centres to divide the data into k clusters.
   - **K-Means++ clustering**
   - **K-Mode clustering**
   - **Fuzzy C-Means (FCM) Clustering**

ii. **Distribution-based Methods**

The main distribution-based techniques are as follows:

- **Gaussian Mixture Models (GMMs):** The model assigns probabilities for the cluster membership of data points by modelling clusters as overlapping Gaussian distributions.
- **Expectation-Maximisation Algorithms**
- **Dirichlet process mixture models (DPMMs)**

iii. **Connectivity Based Methods**

Connectivity based methods are:

- **Hierarchical clustering:** By merging or dividing clusters, hierarchical clustering constructs a dendrogram, a tree-like structure, without a predetermined number.
- **Agglomerative Clustering**
- **Divisive clustering**
- **Affinity propagation**

iv. **Density Based methods**

Density based methods are:

- **DBSCAN (Density-Based Spatial Clustering of Applications with Noise):** Creates density-based clusters using distance and point parameters, allowing for customisable forms and outlier detection.
- **OPTICS (Ordering Points to Identify the Clustering Structure):** OPTICS is a clustering algorithm that identifies density-based clusters in data, handling varying densities by ordering points to reveal clustering structure without explicitly producing a partitioning like DBSCAN.

b) Dimensionality Reduction

Datasets can be made simpler by using dimensionality reduction, which lowers the amount of features while keeping the most crucial information.

i. **Principal Component Analysis (PCA):** Converts information into a fresh collection of principal components, or orthogonal features, that best represent the variance.

ii. **t-distributed Stochastic Neighbour Embedding (t-SNE):** Reduces dimensionality while maintaining local linkages in order to visualise high-dimensional data.

iii. **Non-negative Matrix Factorisation (NMF):** It is helpful for sparse data, such as text or images, to factorise data into non-negative components.

iv. **Isomap:** In order to capture non-linear structures in data, geodesic distances are preserved.

v. **Locally Linear Embedding (LLE):** Local relationships are preserved by reconstructing data points from their neighbours.

vi. **Latent Semantic Analysis (LSA):** Reveals hidden patterns by reducing the dimensionality of text data.

vii. **Autoencoders:** Neural networks are helpful for anomaly detection and feature learning because they can compress and recreate data.

c) Association Rule

Analyse patterns (also known as association rules) among goods in huge datasets, usually in market basket research (e.g., discovering that individuals who purchase bread also buy butter). It finds patterns just by looking at how often items and co-occurrences occur in the dataset.

i. **Apriori algorithm:** Iteratively going through the data and eliminating infrequent item combinations, it finds frequent item-sets.

ii. **FP-Growth (Frequent Pattern-Growth):** Mines frequent item-sets efficiently without the need for candidate generation by employing a compressed FP-tree structure.

iii. **ECLAT (Equivalence Class Clustering and bottom-up Lattice Traversal):** Enables more rapid and frequent pattern finding by effectively intersecting item sets using a vertical data structure.

3. Reinforcement Learning Algorithms

In reinforcement learning, agents are trained to make a series of choices by rewarding good behaviour and punishing poor behaviour. These techniques may be broadly divided into two categories: Model-Based and Model-Free methods. They vary in their interactions with the environment.

a) Model-Based Methods

These techniques simulate possible outcomes using a model of the environment to forecast outcomes and assist the agent in planning actions.

- Markov decision processes (MDPs)
- Bellman equation
- Value iteration algorithm
- Monte Carlo Tree Search

b) Model-Free Methods

These approaches neither create nor depend on an explicit environmental model. By interacting with the environment and modifying its activities in response to input, the agent instead gains firsthand experience. Value-Based and Policy-Based approaches are two more subcategories of model-free approaches:

i. **Value-Based Methods:** Concentrate on learning the values of several states or actions, in which the agent chooses the action with the greatest value after estimating the anticipated return from each one.
   - Q-Learning
   - SARSA
   - Monte Carlo Methods

ii. **Policy-based Methods:** The agent continually modifies its policy to optimise rewards by directly learning a policy (a mapping from states to actions) without guessing values.
   - REINFORCE Algorithm
   - Actor-Critic Algorithm

     o   Asynchronous Advantage Actor-Critic (A3C)

2.4   Data Preprocessing

Data preprocessing, a component of data preparation, refers to any form of processing that is conducted on unprocessed data in order to prepare it for a subsequent data processing procedure. It has long been a crucial first stage in the data mining procedure. Data preparation approaches have been modified more recently for use in training AI and machine learning models as well as for making inferences against them.

To make data mining, machine learning, and other data science operations easier and more efficient, data preprocessing converts the data into a format. To guarantee correct results, the methods are often used at the very beginning of the machine learning and artificial intelligence development process.

Preprocessing data may be done using a variety of tools and techniques, such as the following:

a. Sampling is the process of choosing a representative selection of data from a large population.

b. Transformation creates a single input by modifying raw data.

c. Data noise is eliminated using denoising.

d. Imputation, which fills in missing values with statistically significant data.

e. Normalisation is the process of arranging data for easier access.

f. Feature extraction, which identifies a subset of features that are pertinent and important in a certain situation.

These tools and techniques can be used to a range of data sources, such as streaming data and data saved in files or databases.

1. **Steps For Data Preprocessing**

Figure 2.7: Steps for Data Preprocessing. [7]

The following are some of the steps involved in data preprocessing:

a) **Data Profiling:** The practice of looking at, evaluating, and assessing data in order to get statistics on its quality is known as data profiling.

---

[7]https://www.techtarget.com/rms/onlineimages/steps_for_data_preprocessing-f.png

A study of the current data and its features is the first step. In order to create a hypothesis about characteristics that could be useful for the proposed analytics or machine learning activity, data scientists first discover data sets that are relevant to the issue at hand and then catalogue its significant properties. They also think about which preprocessing libraries may be employed and connect data sources to pertinent business ideas.

b) **Data Cleansing:** In order to ensure that the raw data is appropriate for feature engineering, the goal is to identify the simplest method of fixing quality concerns, such as removing inaccurate data or adding missing data.

c) **Data Reduction:** Raw data sets often include duplicate information that results from characterising occurrences in several ways or information that is unrelated to a certain machine learning, artificial intelligence, or analytics application. Data reduction converts raw data into a more manageable format appropriate for certain use cases by using methods such as principal component analysis.

d) **Data Transformation:** Here, data scientists consider how various data elements might be arranged to best serve the objective. This may encompass the following: the organisation of unstructured data, the integration of salient variables when appropriate, or the identification of critical ranges to concentrate on.

e) **Data Enrichment:** During this stage, data scientists implement the intended transformations by utilising a variety of feature engineering libraries on the data. A data collection structured to strike the best possible balance between the necessary computation and the time needed to train a new model should be the end result.

f) **Data Validation:** The data is now divided into two sets. The first set is employed to train a deep learning or machine learning model. The second set of data is the assessment data, which is employed to evaluate the robustness and accuracy of the final model. This second stage aids in identifying any issues with the hypothesis that was applied to the data's feature engineering and cleaning. Data scientists may assign the preprocessing assignment to a data engineer who will choose how to scale it for production if they are happy with the outcomes. If not, the data scientists have the option to reverse their implementation of the feature engineering and data cleansing stages.

2. **Data Preprocessing Techniques**

Data cleaning and feature engineering are the two primary types of preprocessing. Each has a range of methods, which are explained below:

a) Data Cleansing

The following are some methods for cleaning up jumbled
data:

i. **Identify and sort out missing data:** Individual data
fields may be absent from a data collection for a
number of reasons. Data scientists must determine
whether it is preferable to ignore or reject data with
missing fields or to fill them up with a likely value.
For instance, it could be permissible to add the
missing average temperature between the prior
and subsequent data in an Internet of Things
application that tracks temperature.

ii. **Reduce noisy data:** Analytical or AI models may be
distorted by the noise present in real-world data.
For instance, a sensor that normally records a
temperature of 75 degrees Fahrenheit may indicate
a temperature of 250 degrees instead. The noise
may be reduced using a number of statistical
techniques, including as clustering, regression, and
binning.

iii. **Identify and remove duplicates:** An algorithm
must decide if two seemingly identical recordings
are indeed two independent occurrences or
whether the same measurement was taken twice.
There may sometimes be minor discrepancies in a
record due to an inaccurately reported field. In
other situations, documents that seem to be
duplicates may really be different, such as when a

father and son share a name and reside in the same home but need to be listed as distinct people. These issues may be automatically resolved with the use of duplication detection, removal, or joining techniques.

b) Feature Engineering

The feature engineering refers to methods that data scientists use to arrange the data in ways that facilitate the training of data models and the drawing of conclusions from them. These methods consist of the following:

i. **Feature scaling or normalisation:** The scales at which distinct variables change are often different, or one variable may develop linearly while another changes exponentially. For instance, age is expressed in double digits, but pay may be expressed in thousands of dollars. Scaling aids in transforming the data so that computers may more easily identify a significant correlation between variables.

ii. **Data reduction:** To develop a new AI or analytics model, data scientists often need to integrate data from several sources. It may be safe to exclude some of the variables as they have no correlation with a certain result. In the case of a model that predicts the chance of loan payback, other variables may be meaningful, but only in terms of their connection. For example, the debt-to-credit ratio may be merged into a single variable. In order to reduce the number of dimensions in the training data set and create a more effective representation, methods such as principal component analysis are essential.

iii. **Discretisation:** Raw numbers are often helpfully grouped into distinct intervals. For instance, five categories of income can be identified, each of which would reflect the usual applicants for a certain kind of loan. By doing this, the overhead of drawing inferences against a model or training it may be decreased.

iv. **Feature encoding:** Constructing a structured format out of unstructured data is another facet of feature engineering. Formats for unstructured data might include audio, video, and text. For instance, converting words into numerical vectors using data transformation methods like Word2vec is usually the first step in the development of natural language processing systems. This makes it simple to show the algorithm that, whereas terms like "house" are entirely distinct, "mail" and "parcel" are comparable. Similarly, raw pixel data may be re-encoded into vectors that indicate the separations between various facial features using a facial recognition system.

2.5   Model Evaluation

In the realm of machine learning, evaluating a model entail assessing its predictive accuracy. Predictive accuracy indicates the effectiveness of a model in generating precise predictions for data that has not been previously encountered. The objective is to identify a model that performs effectively on new, previously unencountered examples instead of merely recalling the training data.

Evaluating a model involves more than just measuring its accuracy. Additionally, it includes assessing various factors like the model's capacity to manage class imbalance, its resilience to noisy data, and its capability to address missing values. These elements are essential in assessing a machine learning model's overall effectiveness and dependability.

In the process of evaluating the model, it is typical to divide the available data into sets for training and testing. The model undergoes training using the training set and is subsequently assessed with the testing set to evaluate its performance on data that has not been encountered before. This method aids in simulating real-world situations in which the model must predict outcomes for new, previously unencountered examples.

1. Necessary of Evaluation for a Successful Model

Assessment is essential for confirming that machine learning models are dependable, applicable across various scenarios, and able to produce precise predictions on novel, unencountered data, which is vital for their effective implementation in practical situations. The two main reasons why machine learning algorithms perform poorly are overfitting and underfitting.

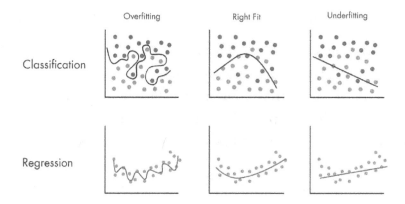

Figure 2.8: Classification and Regression Model. [8]

a. **Overfitting:** Happens when the model is so tightly fitted to the training data that it lacks the ability to react to new data.

b. **Right Fit:** It happens when both the error in the training data and the error in the test data is low.

c. **Underfitting:** Happens when the model fails to sufficiently represent the fundamental framework of the data.

Table 1: Error risks in the models:

Error	Overfitting	Right Fit	Underfitting
Training	Low	Low	High
Test	High	Low	High

---

[8]https://miro.medium.com/v2/resize:fit:828/format:webp/1*cOcV 7J0b-d_MAxStyL-6gg.png

2. The Role of Model Evaluation in Predictive Accuracy

A machine learning model's ultimate objective is to provide precise predictions on actual data. When a model does not successfully forecast results, its value decreases. Evaluating and optimising model performance is essential for success. Understanding the strengths and weaknesses of the models allows for informed decisions regarding their deployment and helps in avoiding potential pitfalls.

Evaluating models assists in recognising and tackling problems like overfitting and underfitting. Overfitting happens when a model shows outstanding performance on the training data yet struggles to apply that knowledge to new data. Underfitting occurs when a model is overly simplistic and does not adequately capture the underlying patterns present in the data. Through the evaluation of the models, it becomes possible to identify and address these issues, thereby ensuring that the models perform effectively on data that has not been previously encountered.

Ultimately, evaluating models represents an essential phase in the machine learning workflow. This enables the assessment of the performance and quality of the models, the understanding of their strengths and weaknesses, and the making of informed decisions regarding their deployment and optimisation. Through the pursuit of predictive accuracy and the resolution of challenges like overfitting and underfitting, reliable and effective machine learning models can be developed to provide accurate predictions on real-world data.

3. Concepts in Model Evaluation

With a clear overview of the significance of model evaluation established, it is time to explore some key concepts that will enhance understanding of the evaluation process.

a) Overfitting and Underfitting

A fundamental concept in model evaluation involves the tradeoff between overfitting and underfitting. Overfitting happens when a model becomes too familiar with the training data, resulting in excessive complexity and a failure to generalise to new instances. Conversely, underfitting occurs when a model is overly simplistic and does not adequately represent the fundamental patterns present in the data. Finding a balance between these two extremes is essential for creating models that demonstrate strong predictive performance on data that has not been previously encountered.

b) Bias-Variance Tradeoff

The bias-variance tradeoff represents a significant factor in the evaluation of models. A model's simplifying assumptions on the connection between the input characteristics and the target variable are referred to as bias. Conversely, variance describes how sensitive the model is to changes in the training set of data. Achieving optimum model performance requires striking the correct balance between variance and bias.

c) Generalisation and Validation

The capability of a model to excel with data that has not been encountered before is referred to as generalisation. This aspect of model evaluation is crucial as it determines the performance of models in real-world scenarios. Validation entails evaluating a model's performance using a distinct validation dataset, comprising instances that were not utilised in the training process. This enables an estimation of the model's ability to generalise to new, unseen examples.

4. Different Types of Model Evaluation Techniques

With a strong grasp of the essential concepts established, the next step involves examining various methods for assessing machine learning models.

a) Holdout Method

The holdout method, referred to as the train-test split, represents one of the most straightforward techniques for model evaluation. The available data is divided into two segments: a training set and a test set. The model undergoes training using the training set and is subsequently assessed using the test set. This enables the estimation of the model's performance on data that has not been previously encountered.

b) Cross-Validation

Cross-validation serves as a more reliable technique for evaluating models, addressing the shortcomings associated with the holdout method. The process entails splitting the data into several subsets or "folds." The model undergoes training using a combination of these folds while being assessed on the fold that remains. A more accurate assessment of the model's performance can be obtained by repeating this procedure with other fold combinations.

c) Bootstrap

Bootstrap is an additional resampling technique that can be implemented for the purpose of model evaluation. This process entails generating several bootstrap samples through the random selection of data from the original dataset, allowing for replacement. A model is trained using each bootstrap sample, and the model's performance is assessed by combining the results from the bootstrap samples.

CHAPTER 3: INTRODUCTION TO DEEP LEARNING

Learning Objective

This chapter explores into Deep Learning, explaining neural networks, various architectures, optimisation techniques, and various challenges. Readers will gain insight into how Deep Learning drives advancements in Generative AI.

3.1 What is Deep Learning

Artificial neural networks are used in deep learning, a subset of machine learning, to extract knowledge from data. Artificial neural networks, which draw inspiration from the human brain, can be used to a broad range of applications, such as voice recognition, picture identification, and natural language processing.

1. Deep Learning Algorithms

Large labelled data sets are often used to train deep learning systems. The algorithms are trained to assign the appropriate labels to the data's characteristics. As an instance, in an image recognition job, the algorithm may learn to link certain aspects in a picture (such an object's form or colour) to the appropriate label (like "dog" or "cat").

A deep learning system is capable of making predictions on fresh data once it has been learnt. For instance, dogs in fresh photographs can be recognised using a deep learning system that has been taught to recognise dog images.

2. Working of Deep Learning

A neural network processes incoming data by working together with layers of linked nodes, or neurones. Data moves through many layers in a fully connected deep neural network, where each neurone carries out nonlinear modifications to enable the model to learn complex data representations.

Data enters a deep neural network via the input layer and then travels through hidden layers that use nonlinear functions to alter the data. The model's forecast is produced by the last output layer.

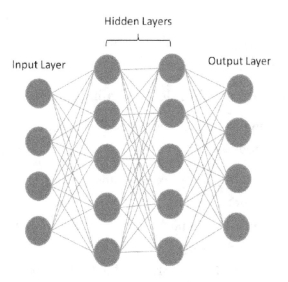

Figure 3.1: Fully Connected Deep Neural Network.

3. Types of Deep Learning

Deep learning models come in a variety of forms. The following are among the most prevalent types:

a) Convolutional Neural Networks (CNNs)

CNNs are used to analyse and recognise images. They are very adept at recognising items in pictures, even if they are deformed or partly hidden.

b) Deep Reinforcement Learning

Deep reinforcement learning is used to gaming and robotics. This kind of machine learning enables an agent to interact with an environment and learn how to behave by getting rewards or penalties.

c) Recurrent Neural Networks (RNNs)

Speech recognition and natural language processing are two applications of RNNs. In addition to being able to create text and translate languages, they excel in comprehending the context of a sentence or phrase.

4. Benefits of Using Deep Learning Models

The following are some benefits of employing deep learning models:

a. **Learning complex relationships between features in data:** They are thus more potent than conventional machine learning techniques.
b. **Large dataset training:** As a result, they may learn from a greater variety of events and become more scalable, resulting in more precise forecasts.

    c. **Data-driven learning:** DL models are more efficient and scalable since they can learn from data and need less human interaction during training. Continuously produced data, such that from sensors or social media, is used to train these models.

5. **Deep Learning Applications**

Application areas for deep learning are many and include:

    a. **Image recognition:** To recognise characteristics and things in pictures, including people, animals, locations, etc.

    b. **Natural language processing:** To aid with text comprehension, as in spam filters and chatbots for customer support.

    c. **Finance:** To aid in the analysis of financial data and the forecasting of market changes.

    d. **Text to image**: Use a tool like Google Translate to convert text into pictures.

3.2   Neural Networks

Neural networks are models for machine learning that replicate the intricate processes of the human brain. These models are made up of linked neurones or nodes that process information, recognise patterns, and make it possible to perform tasks like pattern recognition and decision-making.

Neural networks don't need pre-established rules to learn and recognise patterns in data. These networks are constructed using a number of essential components:

a. **Neurons**: Each neuron, the fundamental units that accept inputs, is controlled by an activation function and a threshold.

b. **Connections**: Information-carrying connections between neurons that are controlled by weights and biases.

c. **Weights and Biases**: The strength and impact of linkages are determined by these factors.

d. **Propagation Functions**: Mechanisms that facilitate data processing and transmission between neuronal layers.

e. **Learning Rule**: The technique that gradually modifies biases and weights to increase accuracy.

Neural networks use an organised, three-step learning process:

a. **Input Computation**: The network is fed data.

b. **Output Generation**: The network produces an output based on the parameters that are currently in place.

c. **Iterative Refinement**: The network continually improves its performance on a variety of tasks by fine-tuning its output by modifying weights and biases.

A simulated scenario or dataset is presented to the neural network in an adaptive learning environment. In reaction to fresh information or circumstances, parameters like weights and biases are modified. The network's reaction changes with each modification, enabling it to successfully respond to various tasks or circumstances.

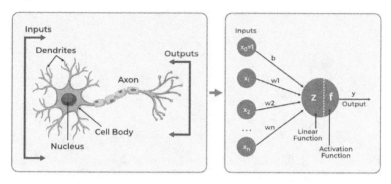

Figure 3.2: The analogy between a biological neuron and an artificial neuron. [9]

1. Importance of Neural Networks

Neural networks are essential for recognising nuanced patterns, resolving difficult problems, and adjusting to changing conditions. Their capacity to learn from enormous volumes of data is revolutionary, influencing automated decision-making, self-driving cars, and natural language processing, among other technologies.

Neural networks improve productivity, facilitate decision-making, and simplify procedures in a variety of sectors.

---

[9]https://media.geeksforgeeks.org/wp-content/uploads/20241106171024318092/Artificial-Neural-Networks.webp

They continue to spur innovation and influence the direction of technology as the foundation of artificial intelligence.

2. Layers in Neural Network Architecture

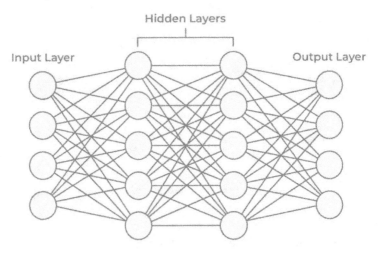

Figure 3.3: Layers in Neural Network Architecture. [10]

The layers of a neural network architecture are as follows:

a. **Input Layer:** The network gets its input data from this source. A feature in the input data is represented by each input neurone in the layer.

b. **Hidden Layers:** The majority of the computational hard lifting is done by these levels. One or more hidden layers may be present in a neural network. The inputs are converted into something the output

---

[10]https://ayarlabs.com/wp-content/uploads/2023/01/Neural-Network-Architecture.jpg

layer can utilise by the units (neurons) that make up each layer.

c. **Output Layer:** The model's output is generated by the last layer. Depending on the particular goal (e.g., classification, regression), these outputs have different formats.

3. **Types of Neural Networks**

There are distinct varieties of neural networks eligible for implementation.

a. **Feedforward Networks:** A feedforward neural network is a basic artificial neural network design where information flows in a single path from input to output.

b. **Multilayer Perceptron (MLP):** One or more hidden layers, an input layer, and an output layer make up an MLP, a kind of feedforward neural network. Activation functions that are nonlinear are used.

c. **Convolutional Neural Network (CNN):** An artificial neural network specifically developed for image processing is called a convolutional neural network. Convolutional layers are used to automatically extract hierarchical characteristics from input photos, allowing for efficient image classification and identification.

d. **Recurrent Neural Network (RNN):** Recurrent neural networks (RNNs) are a form of artificial neural network designed for sequential data processing. Since it uses feedback loops, which allow information to persist inside the network, it is suitable for applications like time series prediction and natural language processing where contextual dependencies are crucial.

e. **Long Short-Term Memory (LSTM):** An RNN type called LSTM was created to solve the vanishing gradient issue in RNN training. Information can be read, written, and erased selectively using memory cells and gates.

3.3 Deep Learning Architectures

Deep learning architectures have undergone substantial changes over time, as a result of improvements in computational capacity, data availability, and research. They are a significant breakthrough in artificial intelligence (AI), drawing inspiration from the neural networks found in the human brain to provide robots life-changing powers. Understanding the crucial components of deep learning architectures might make the process easier, even if they are complex:

a) **Neurons:** Neurons, the basic building blocks of neural networks, process inputs, assign weights, and generate outputs in a manner similar to that of brain neurons.

b) **Activation Functions:** These factors determine whether a neuron activates. For instance, the ReLU (Rectified Linear Unit) function activates a neurone by passing positive input values and outputting zero for negative inputs, thereby influencing the neuron's response.

c) **Weights and Biases:** Adaptable parameters that set activation thresholds and affect the significance of input features. Biases provide the minimal condition for activation, while weights show the importance of a feature. These settings are changed throughout training to increase accuracy.

d) **Loss Functions:** They direct the training process by quantifying the discrepancy between expected and actual outcomes. The objective is to reduce this disparity, and typical loss functions include Cross-Entropy Loss and Mean Squared Error (MSE).

e) **Optimizers:** Optimisers are essential for fine-tuning model parameters to reduce loss and improve performance by modifying weights and biases depending on loss. Popular methods include RMSprop, Adam, and Stochastic Gradient Descent (SGD).

These fundamental ideas enable to explore increasingly elaborate deep learning architectures, in which many layers of neurons collaborate to resolve challenging issues.

Let's examine a few of the most popular and significant models in the field of deep learning, each with special advantages and uses.

1. Recurrent Neural Networks (RNNs)

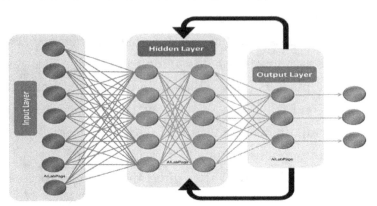

Figure 3.4: Recurrent Neural Networks (RNNs). [11]

The fundamental deep-learning architectures known as RNNs are designed to process sequential input. They are perfect for tasks like voice recognition because they analyse variable-length input sequences using their internal state, or memory. RNNs are particularly helpful in domains like machine translation, voice synthesis, and natural language processing (NLP) where the order of information is essential. There are two popular kinds of RNNs:

    a. **Bidirectional RNNs:** The output layer may concurrently receive information from past and future states by processing data both forward and backward.

---

[11]https://miro.medium.com/v2/resize:fit:1200/0*Pd26UtIt3uxhqH7A.png

b. **Deep RNNs:** They are capable of extracting additional hierarchical information from the data due to the presence of multiple layers.

2. **Convolutional Neural Networks (CNNs)**

Drawing inspiration from the visual brain of animals, Yann LeCun was the first to develop this multilayer neural network. The architecture was first created for applications such as postal code interpretation and handwritten character recognition. Convolutional neural networks, or CNNs, are now crucial for classification and image processing. Important layers consist of:

a. **Convolutional Layer:** Features are extracted using kernels, with ReLU activation added for non-linearity.

b. **Pooling Layer:** Reduces dimensionality while maintaining important information by using maximum or average pooling.

c. **Fully Connected Layer:** Connects every input to every neuron to complete the categorisation.

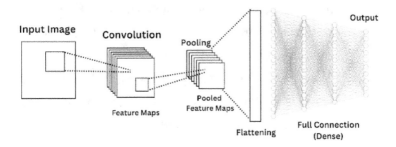

Figure 3.5: CNN Architecture.

CNN functionality is improved by additional components such as dropout layers to avoid overfitting and softmax activation for output normalisation. CNNs are essential in many different sectors because of their superior performance in applications such as object identification, face recognition, medical imaging, natural language processing, and more.

3. Long Short-Term Memory (LSTM)

Hochreiter and Schimdhuber developed LSTM in 1997, and it has been more and more well-liked as an RNN architecture for a variety of applications in recent years. LSTMs are sophisticated RNNs that overcome the drawbacks of conventional RNNs by capturing long-range relationships in sequential data. Important features include:

a. **Memory Cells:** Long-term information retention that captures dependencies and context in sequential data.

b. **Gates:** To ensure efficient information retention and disposal, three gates—input, forget, and output—control the flow of data into and out of memory cells.

c. **Vanishing Gradient Problem:** LSTMs effectively learn long-term dependencies by maintaining a steady error flow over time.

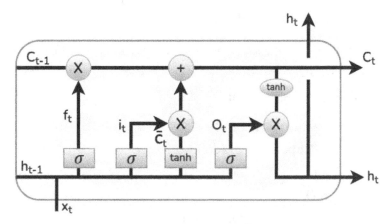

Figure 3.6: LSTM Working. [12]

4.   Gated Recurrent Unit (GRU)

GRUs are a more computationally efficient and simpler form of LSTMs that improve long-term dependency modelling. Important features include:

a. **Gating Mechanism:** Information flow in the network is managed by two gates: update and reset. The update gate controls the percentage of data that should be kept or discarded, while the reset gate controls when the internal state should be reset.

b. **Simplicity:** GRUs are appropriate for applications such as time series prediction, voice recognition, and natural language processing (NLP) because they need fewer parameters and train faster.

---

[12]https://media.geeksforgeeks.org/wp-content/uploads/20240208053129/lstm.webp

5. ResNet (Residual Networks)

ResNet is a well-known deep learning architecture that uses residual modules to create very deep networks. Among the major advances are:

a. **Residual Modules:** To mitigate the issue of disappearing gradients, either perform a series of functions on the input or omit the step completely.

b. **SGD:** Use an acceptable initialisation function and ordinary stochastic gradient descent.

c. **Preprocessing:** Prior to being fed into the network, inputs are separated into patches.

6. Generative Adversarial Networks (GANs)

GANs learn and produce new data that is similar to the original dataset, making them effective models for generative tasks. Essential components consist of:

a. **Generator:** Aims to provide realistic results by generating new data instances from random inputs.

b. **Discriminator:** Serves to differentiate between produced and actual data by acting as a classifier.

c. **Adversarial Training:** The discriminator and generator train concurrently and competitively. Applications include text-based picture creation, virtual reality, and image generation. Conditional GANs (cGANs) improve specificity by producing data depending on auxiliary information.

7. Transformer Architecture

A revolutionary encoder-decoder architecture, transformers were introduced by Vaswani et al. in 2017. Transformers, in contrast to conventional RNNs, use self-attention processes to assess the relative relevance of various sequence parts, enabling quicker training and parallel processing. Among the applications are:

a. **NLP Tasks:** Sentiment analysis, text summarisation, and machine translation. Transformers are used in models such as BERT to enhance contextual comprehension by taking into account both the left and right context during pre-training.

8. **Deep Belief Network (DBN)**

Stacked Restricted Boltzmann Machines (RBMs) make up DBNs, which are multilayer networks. With DBNs learning complete input probabilities via unsupervised learning, each pair of linked layers becomes an RBM. DBNs do very well on tasks like image recognition and natural language processing (NLP) because to their all-encompassing approach.

9. **Deep Stacking Network (DSN)**

Deep Convex Networks (DCN), another name for DSNs, are made up of many separate deep networks, each of which has hidden layers. This architecture views training as a collection of issues in order to solve the complexity of conventional deep-learning models. The modular stacking used by DSNs, which consists of input, hidden, and output layers in each module, increases training efficiency.

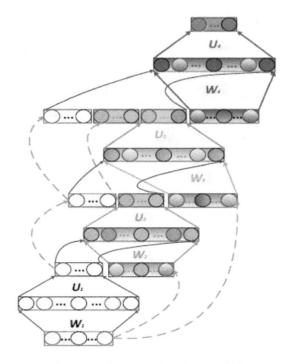

Figure 3.7: Deep Stacking Network. [13]

3.4 Optimisation Techniques

A branch of machine learning called deep learning handles complex tasks like text categorisation and audio recognition. Deep learning models, which include hidden layers, input, output, activation functions, and loss functions, are designed to generalise data and provide predictions on previously unknown data. Several methods,

---

[13]https://www.researchgate.net/publication/333997546/figure/fig 2/AS:773656443637761@1561465478170/DSN-Deep-Stacking-Network.ppm

referred to as optimisers, are used to maximise these models. Neural networks may learn from data thanks to optimisers that repeatedly change model parameters during training in order to minimise a loss function.

Optimisers are essential for improving accuracy and expediting the training process, which shapes deep learning models' overall performance.

1. Gradient Descent

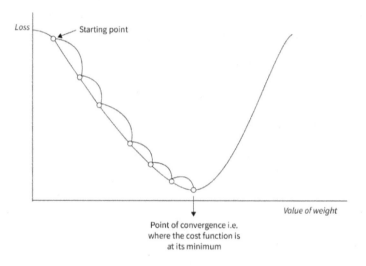

Figure 3.8: Gradient Descent. [14]

A simple optimisation technique called gradient descent modifies the model's parameters in order to reduce the loss function. The algorithm's fundamental form can be expressed as follows:

---

[14]https://www.scaler.com/topics/images/gradient-descents.webp

$$\theta = \theta - \alpha \cdot \nabla\theta L(\theta)$$

Where

- θ is the model parameter,
- $L(\theta)$) is the loss function, and
- α is the learning rate.

2. Stochastic Gradient Descent

Stochastic gradient descent (SGD) represents a variation of gradient descent that updates parameters using a small, randomly chosen subset of the data, known as a "mini-batch," instead of utilising the entire dataset. The basic form of the algorithm can be written as follows:

$$\theta = \theta - \alpha \cdot \nabla\theta L(\theta; x^{(i)}; y^{(i)})$$

Where $(x^{(i)}, y^{(i)})$ is a mini-batch of data.

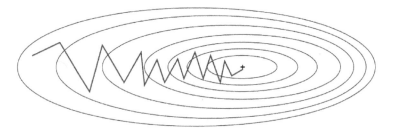

Figure 3.9: Stochastic Gradient Descent. [15]

3. Stochastic Gradient Descent with Momentum

---

[15]https://www.scaler.com/topics/images/stochastic-gradient-descent.webp

SGD with momentum represents a variation of SGD that incorporates a "momentum" component into the update rule, aiding the optimiser in maintaining its trajectory even when the local gradient is minimal. The momentum term is generally assigned a value ranging from 0 to 1. The update rule can be expressed as follows:

$$v=\beta \cdot v+(1-\beta) \cdot \nabla\theta L(\theta;x^{(i)};y^{(i)})$$

$$\theta=\theta-\alpha \cdot v$$

Where

- v is the momentum vector and
- β is the momentum hyperparameter.

SGD without momentum   **SGD with momentum**

Figure 3.10: Stochastic Gradient Descent with Momentum. [16]

4. Mini-Batch Gradient Descent

Mini-batch gradient descent resembles stochastic gradient descent; however, it utilises a small, fixed-size group of samples to calculate the gradient rather than relying on a single sample. The update rule remains consistent with that of SGD, with the exception that the gradient is

---

[16]https://www.scaler.com/topics/images/sgd-with-momentum.webp

averaged across the mini-batch. This has the potential to minimise noise in the updates and enhance convergence.

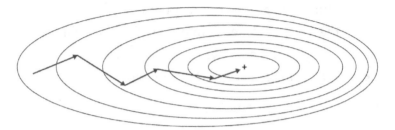

Figure 3.11: Mini-Batch Gradient Descent. [17]

5.   Adagrad

An optimisation algorithm known as Adagrad employs an adaptive learning rate for each parameter. The learning rate is adjusted according to historical gradient information, resulting in parameters that undergo frequent updates having a reduced learning rate, while those that experience fewer updates have an increased learning rate. The update rule can be expressed in the following manner:

$$g = \nabla \theta L(\theta; x^{(i)}; y^{(i)})$$

$$G = G + g \odot g$$

$$\theta = \theta - \alpha / G + \square \odot g$$

Where

- G is a matrix that accumulates the squares of the gradients, and
- ϵ is a small constant added to avoid division by zero.

6. RMSProp

RMSProp is an optimisation algorithm that resembles Adagrad; however, it employs an exponentially decaying average of the squares of the gradients instead of the sum. This assists in diminishing the consistent learning rate decline of Adagrad and enhances convergence. The update rule can be expressed in the following manner:

$$g=\nabla\theta L(\theta;x^{(i)};y^{(i)})$$

$$G=\beta\cdot G+(1-\beta)\cdot g\odot g$$

$$\theta=\theta-\alpha/G+\epsilon\odot g$$

Where

- G is a matrix that accumulates the squares of the gradients,
- ϵ is a small constant added to avoid division by zero, and
- β is a decay rate hyperparameter.

7. AdaDelta

AdaDelta is an optimisation algorithm that resembles RMSProp, yet it does not necessitate a hyperparameter learning rate. Rather, it employs an exponentially decaying average of the gradients along with the squares of the gradients to establish the updated scale. The update rule can be expressed in the following manner:

$$g = \nabla_\theta L(\theta; x^{(i)}; y^{(i)})$$

$$G = \beta \cdot G + (1 - \beta) \cdot g \odot g$$

$$\Delta\theta = -\frac{\sqrt{S+\epsilon}}{\sqrt{G+\epsilon}} \odot g$$

$$S = \beta \cdot S + (1 - \beta) \cdot \Delta\theta \odot \Delta\theta$$

$$\theta = \theta + \Delta\theta$$

Where

- G and S are matrices that accumulate the gradients and the squares of the updates, respectively, and
- ϵ is a small constant added to avoid division.

8. Adam

The optimisation approach known as Adam (short for adaptive moment estimation) blends the concepts of SGD with momentum and RMSProp. Similar to RMSProp, it determines the updated scale by averaging the gradients and their squares exponentially. Additionally, a momentum term is used to aid the optimiser in navigating the loss function more effectively. The following is one way to write the update rule:

$$g = \nabla_\theta L(\theta; x^{(i)}; y^{(i)})$$

$$m = \beta_1 \cdot m + (1 - \beta_1) \cdot g$$

$$v = \beta_2 \cdot v + (1 - \beta_2) \cdot g \odot g$$

$$\hat{m} = \frac{m}{1 - \beta_1^t}$$

$$\hat{v} = \frac{v}{1 - \beta_2^t}$$

$$\theta = \theta - \frac{\alpha}{\sqrt{\hat{v} + \epsilon}} \odot \hat{m}$$

Where

- m and v are the momentum and velocity vectors, respectively, and
- $\beta 1$ and $\beta 2$ are decay rates for the momentum and velocity.

3.5 Challenges in Deep Learning

Deep learning has a lot of promise, but there are a few obstacles that might prevent it from being used effectively. Developing dependable and effective models requires addressing these issues. The following are the main challenges in deep learning:

1. Overfitting and Underfitting

It might be difficult to balance model complexity such that it performs effectively when applied to fresh data. Overfitting is a phenomenon that arises when a model is overly intricate and incorporates noise in the training data. A model that is too simplistic and misses the underlying patterns is said to be underfit.

2. Data Quality and Quantity

For training, deep learning models need big, high-quality datasets. Inaccurate forecasts and model failures may result from inadequate or subpar data. Large dataset acquisition and annotation may be costly and time-consuming.

3. Computational Resources

Deep learning model training requires a large amount of processing power and resources. For many organisations, this might be costly and unavailable. In order to manage the demanding calculations, high-performance hardware such as GPUs and TPUs is often required.

4. Interpretability

Deep learning models are often "black boxes," meaning it's difficult to comprehend how they arrive at conclusions. This lack of openness can be troublesome, particularly in applications that are crucial. For accountability and trust to exist, it is essential to comprehend the decision-making process.

5. Hyperparameter Tuning

It takes skill to determine the best hyperparameter values for a model. This procedure may need a lot of calculation and time. The model's performance is greatly influenced by its hyperparameters, and attaining high accuracy requires careful adjustment.

6. Scalability

A significant obstacle is scaling deep learning models to effectively manage big datasets and challenging tasks. It often takes considerable alterations to ensure models function properly in practical situations. In order to handle growing loads, this entails optimising infrastructure and algorithms.

7. Ethical and Bias Issues

It is possible for deep learning algorithms to unintentionally pick up on and reinforce biases found in training data. This can result in ethical concerns and unjust outcomes. For models to be accepted and seen as reliable, bias must be addressed and fairness must be guaranteed.

8. Hardware Limitations

Significant computing resources, such as high-performance GPUs or TPUs, are needed for deep learning model training. For researchers and practitioners, having access to such gear may be a barrier.

9. Adversarial Attacks

Deep learning algorithms are vulnerable to adversarial assaults, in which misclassification results from minute changes to the input data. Robustness against such assaults is still a major problem in applications that are crucial to safety.

CHAPTER 4: GENERATIVE MODELS

Learning Objective

This chapter explores generative models, differentiating them from discriminative models, and introduces latent variables, Bayesian methods, and data simulation. It provides a deep dive into the mathematical foundations of Generative AI.

4.1 Why Generative Models?

A generative model generates representations or abstractions of observable events or target variables using statistical and probabilistic techniques together with artificial intelligence (AI). New data that resembles the observed data may then be produced using these representations.

Computers can comprehend the actual world by using generative modelling in unsupervised machine learning (ML) to characterise occurrences in data. From modelled data, this AI comprehension can be employed to infer a wide range of probabilities regarding a subject.

1. Working of Generative Models

Neural networks are often used to run generative models. Usually, a big data collection is needed to build a generative model. Several instances from the data set are fed into the model during training, and its parameters are changed to better fit the data distribution.

The learnt distribution can be sampled by the model to provide fresh data once it has been trained. The data that is generated may resemble the original data set, but it may contain some noise or variations. For instance, a model that can create a new image of a horse that has never been but yet seems almost realistic may be developed using a data collection of pictures of horses. This is made feasible by the model's acquisition of the broad guidelines governing a horse's look.

Generative models may also be utilised in many other applications, including data augmentation, picture and voice production, and unsupervised learning to find underlying patterns and structure in unlabelled data.

2. Types of Generative Models

The most common kinds of generative models are as follows:

a) Generative Adversarial Network (GAN)

Deep neural networks and machine learning form the basis of this concept. It involves a competition between two unstable neural networks, a discriminator and a generator, to provide more realistic data and predictions.

An unsupervised learning method called a GAN enables the automated discovery and learning of various patterns in input data. Image-to-image translation, which converts daylight photographs into nighttime photos, is one of its primary applications. Additionally, GANs are utilised to produce very realistic representations of a wide range of items, people, and settings that are difficult for even the human brain to distinguish as fake.

b) Variational Autoencoders (VAEs)

VAEs are generative models that are built on neural network autoencoders, which are made up of encoders and decoders, two distinct neural networks, much like GANs. They're the most effective and useful way to create generative models.

In order to swiftly sample fresh data from the training data's underlying probability distribution, VAE, a probabilistic graphical model based on Bayesian inference, aims to comprehend that distribution. The encoders in VAEs seek to better represent the data, while the decoders more effectively reconstruct the original data set. VAEs are often used in signal processing, security analytics, and anomaly detection for predictive maintenance.

c) Autoregressive Models

Autoregressive models may readily accommodate a range of time-series patterns and forecast future values based on previous values. These models use a linear combination of a sequence's historical values to forecast its future values.

Forecasting and the study of time series, including stock prices and index values, often use autoregressive models. Modelling and predicting weather trends, predicting product demand based on historical sales data, and

researching crime and health effects are some further use
examples.

d) Bayesian Networks

Graphical representations of probabilistic interactions
between variables are called Bayesian networks. They do
very well in circumstances when knowledge of cause and
effect is essential. For example, based on observed
symptoms, a Bayesian network may efficiently determine
the likelihood of a disease in medical diagnosis.

e) Diffusion Models

Noise is gradually introduced into diffusion models,
which subsequently learn to reverse the process. This
results in the generation of data.

They are essential for comprehending the evolution of
phenomena and are especially helpful in examining
scenarios like the spread of infectious illnesses within a
population or the propagation of rumours in social
networks.

f) Restricted Boltzmann Machines

RBMs are neural networks with two layers that can learn
the input data's probability distribution. They are used in
recommendation systems, which utilise user preferences to
offer films on streaming platforms.

g) Pixel Recurrent Neural Networks

One kind of generative model intended for picture
generating applications is PixelRNNs. They are

particularly trained to model pictures pixel by pixel in order to produce new images that match the ones in the training data. They are based on the idea of recurrent neural networks.

h) Markov Chains

Generative models known as Markov chains ignore previous states and predict future states only based on the present state. In text generation, they are often used to anticipate the subsequent word in a phrase based just on the word that is now being used.

i) Normalising Flows

These generative models may describe real-world data by converting a basic, readily sampled probability distribution—like a Gaussian distribution—into a more intricate distribution.

Applying a sequence of invertible transformations on a basic distribution with the goal of producing a distribution that closely resembles the target data distribution is the main objective of normalising flows.

4.2   Generative vs Discriminative Models

In machine learning, knowing the distinction between discriminative and generative models is essential for choosing the best strategy to address certain issues. Models of these two categories are frequently pitted against one another in order to achieve optimal performance. Generative models, like Naive Bayes and

Generative Adversarial Networks (GANs), concentrate on creating new data instances and modelling the distribution of data. Discriminative models, on the other hand, such as Support Vector Machines (SVMs) and Logistic Regression, learn to differentiate between data classes by concentrating on boundaries.

1. Generative Model

A subfield of artificial intelligence (AI) called "generative AI" is dedicated to producing original content, such prose, music, and graphics. One kind of machine learning model that seeks to comprehend the underlying distributions and patterns of data is called a generative model. After learning from the data, it may produce brand-new data that is comparable to the original data.

Generative AI carefully examines information to identify complex linkages and traits that are present. This is known as AI training. For instance, the AI model may be trained on a billion old writings to produce an essay. This includes a wide range of media, including code, text, pictures, and music.

It then starts creating new data instances that are similar to those in the original dataset. Furthermore, probabilistic methods are often used in generative AI to simulate the underlying data distributions. It can accurately determine the probability of the many outputs it produces in this way, guaranteeing a realistic result.

2. Discriminative Model

Conditional models, also known as discriminative models, are another kind of machine learning model that has several applications. Classification challenges are a typical illustration of discriminative AI. The AI model is taught to categorise inputs into pre-established groups.

A discriminative AI example might be a spam email filter. The classification of emails as spam or not spam is determined by factors such as the structure of the email, the originator information, and the keywords used.

Discriminative AI functions via a unique mechanism that mostly involves the algorithms used and the training procedure. First, tagged data is used to train these models. Their respective categories are indicated by the specific class identifiers that are assigned to each data point. The model can more easily identify key characteristics that act as class discriminators thanks to this tagged data. Second, a range of algorithms are necessary for discriminative AI to operate. Examples of these include the well-known logistic regression, neural networks, decision trees, and support vector machines (SVMs). Depending on how it was trained and how the algorithm is configured, discriminative AI may now distinguish between spam and relevant emails and assist with data analytics.

3. Generative Models Vs Discriminative Models: Comparison Summary

The main distinctions and similarities between generative and discriminative models are succinctly summarised in this table. It outlines each of their goals, methods of instruction, uses, advantages, and disadvantages.

Aspect	Generative Models	Discriminative Models
Objective	"Learn joint probability distribution of data	"Learn conditional probability of target given data
Focus	Generate new data samples	Make predictions/classifications based on data
Training Approach	Typically unsupervised learning	Typically supervised learning
Example Applications	Image generation, text generation, data augmentation	Classification, regression, sequence labeling
Key Algorithms	Variational Autoencoders (VAEs), Generative Adversarial Networks (GANs)	Convolutional Neural Networks (CNNs), Recurrent Neural Networks (RNNs), Support Vector Machines (SVMs)

Strengths	Can create new data, capture data distribution	Precise predictions, efficient training
Weaknesses	Requires large datasets, mode collapse (in GANs)	Limited understanding of data distribution, can overfit
Use in Deep Learning	Data generation, anomaly detection."	Classification, regression."

4.3   Latent Variables

A latent variable is, to put it simply, an unobservable or hidden variable that affects observed data. These variables are inferred using mathematical models that connect them to observable data, rather than being explicitly quantifiable. As an example, consider a concept of intelligence. Measurable markers like exam scores, problem-solving ability, and decision-making skills may be used to infer intelligence, even when it cannot be directly witnessed or evaluated. In this instance, intelligence is a latent variable.

1.   Types of Latent Variables

In general, latent variables fall into one of two categories:

a. **Continuous Latent Variables:** These are variables that are not observable but have continuous values. A few examples are health, intelligence, or socioeconomic status. In probabilistic models such as Factor Analysis and Gaussian Mixture Models (GMM), continuous latent variables are often used in machine learning.

b. **Categorical Latent Variables**: Discrete categories or groupings are represented by these unobservable variables. For example, a person's personality type (extrovert, introvert) or mood (happy, sad, and neutral) might be considered categorical latent variables. Models like Hidden Markov Models (HMMs) and Latent Class Analysis (LCA) often employ these kinds of variables.

2. **Importance of Latent Variables in Modelling**

In a number of fields, latent variables are essential because they make complicated models easier to understand and reveal the underlying patterns that underlie observable data. Latent variables have importance in a number of crucial domains, including:

a. **Psychometrics:** Latent variables are utilised in educational and psychological testing to determine personality characteristics, motivation, anxiety, and intelligence levels. Latent variables in IQ testing, for instance, indicate the degree of intelligence deduced from performance on different tasks.

b. **Social Sciences**: Latent variables are used by researchers to examine intricate concepts such as social standing, attitudes, and beliefs. In the social sciences, structural equation modelling, or SEM, is a widely used technique for examining the links between observable and unobserved factors using latent variables.

c. **Machine Learning**: Latent variables are used in unsupervised learning models, such as Principal Component Analysis (PCA), to capture underlying characteristics or dimensions in high-dimensional data, such text or picture analysis. Latent variables are essential to deep learning because they aid in representing compressed representations of input data in Autoencoders and Variational Autoencoders (VAEs).

d. **Economics:** Concepts that are not immediately quantifiable but have an impact on observable economic behaviour, such as consumer preferences or market emotion, are described by latent variables in economic modelling.

3. **Benefits of Using Latent Variables**

The primary benefits of employing latent variables are as follows:

a. **Simplification of Complex Models**: Researchers and data scientists may identify underlying patterns that explain intricate interactions in the data by using latent variables. This lowers the complexity of the data and produces models that are easier to understand.

b. **Increased Model Accuracy:** Models that include latent variables often provide more accurate estimates or forecasts by taking hidden elements into consideration.

c. **Theoretical Insight:** Latent variables provide a better understanding of human behaviour, social trends, or hidden patterns in data by shedding light on theoretical concepts and abstract constructs that are impossible to measure directly.

4.4   Bayesian Methods

In artificial intelligence, Bayesian Machine Learning (BML) is a complex paradigm that combines machine learning with the strength of statistical inference. BML presents the idea of probability and inference, providing a framework where learning changes as evidence mounts, in contrast to classical machine learning, which mostly concentrates on predictions.

Integrating new data with existing knowledge is the foundation of BML. This fusion results in a model that is more complex and that is constantly evolving. For example, a BML system may know in advance that a patient exhibiting certain symptoms is likely to develop the flu. It improves its knowledge and forecasts about flu diagnosis when additional patient data becomes available.

The focus on probability and inference sets BML apart from its more conventional cousins. BML performs best when the data is scarce but the model is complicated, while classical machine learning performs best when the data is plentiful. According to Wolfram's introduction to Bayesian Inference, here is where Bayesian inference becomes an essential tool, offering a rigorous and understandable approach to statistical analysis.

In order to calculate conditional probabilities—the chance of an event happening given the occurrence of another event—BML fundamentally uses Bayes' Theorem. This statistical foundation allows BML to provide forecasts that are probabilistically informed claims rather than just educated guesses.

The following three components are essential to Bayesian analysis:

a. **Prior:** The original opinion prior to taking fresh information into account.

b. **Likelihood:** The likelihood of seeing the new evidence under different theories.

c. **Posterior:** The revised belief in light of the fresh information.

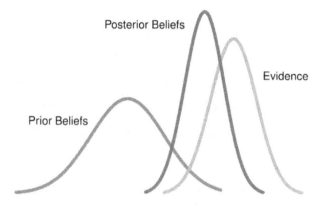

Figure 4.1: Bayesian analysis components. [18]

This methodology enables BML to provide predictions that are resilient and versatile, especially when working with sparse or small datasets, which may be challenging for standard machine learning.

A group of methods and algorithms known as Bayesian Machine Learning (BML) use Bayesian principles to describe data uncertainty. These techniques are useful tools that have revolutionised how robots learn from data; they are not only theoretical concepts.

1. Probabilistic Programming

In BML, probabilistic programming is essential because it serves as a link between statistical theory and computer application. It makes it possible for data scientists to

---

[18]https://deepgram.com/_next/image?url=https%3A%2F%2Fww
w.datocms-assets.com%2F96965%2F1707230263-ai-apps-
bayesianml-image-1.png&w=1080&q=75

simplify the intricate process of Bayesian inference by encoding models with rich probabilistic semantics. The importance of such tools, which can manage the complexities of BML with grace and speed, is highlighted in the Wolfram introduction to Bayesian Inference.

2. Probabilistic Graphical Models

BML excels in the field of probabilistic graphical models, which allow dependencies in data to be visually and understandably represented. These models are strong because they enable predictions and conclusions that are based on a thorough comprehension of the underlying connections, in addition to capturing the core of the structure of the data.

3. Bayesian Program Learning (BPL)

By enabling computers to extrapolate beyond the provided data, Bayesian Program Learning advances BML. Imagining new possibilities that help improve the learning process is similar to providing the system an imagination that is based on statistical likelihood. The capacity to produce supplementary examples is especially advantageous in industries where data is scarce or costly to acquire.

4. Common Bayesian Models

The mainstays of BML are Bayesian Networks, Gaussian Processes, and Dirichlet Processes. Data scientists use these models, each with unique capabilities, as building blocks to create complex learning systems that can solve a variety of issues.

5. Markov Chain Monte Carlo (MCMC) Methods

BML relies on Markov Chain Monte Carlo techniques to overcome the computational difficulties of inference. MCMC techniques allow for the approximation of posteriors that would be impractical to compute directly by sampling from complicated distributions, particularly as the dimensionality of the data increases.

6. Bayesian Hyperparameter Optimisation

In machine learning, hyperparameter optimisation is a crucial stage, and the Bayesian approach adds a degree of complexity that is unmatched by conventional techniques. It offers new opportunities for efficiency and performance improvements by approaching hyperparameter tweaking as a Bayesian inference issue.

4.5   Data Simulation

Data simulation is the process of creating artificial data that closely resembles the features and attributes of actual data. Data scientists, engineers, and commercial enterprises can access training data at a fraction of the cost thanks to the benefit of simulated data, which is produced using mathematical or computational models rather than surveys, monitoring software, or website scraping.

1. Data Simulation Features

Complex systems may be tested and validated using simulated data before being applied to real data. Under ideal circumstances, simulated data may be used to verify the accuracy and quality of an analytics system because it is comprehensive and seldom contains errors or gaps. All of this can be accomplished with real-world data, but data simulation is far less expensive and does not include the ethical and regulatory issues that come with managing and retaining user data.

Beyond its cost, data simulations appeal to people, groups, and businesses that deal with data for a variety of reasons. Three primary categories may be used to evaluate its features: replicability, scalability, and flexibility.

a. **Flexibility:** Since the data is artificial, it may be modified to replicate a variety of situations and circumstances without moral limitations, enabling a system to be examined in more detail. This is very helpful for evaluating predictive and large-scale simulation models. It also helps with sophisticated data visualisation, enabling accuracy testing under harsh circumstances.

b. **Scalability:** Data volume is just as important as data quality when it comes to training AI and machine learning models. Since simulated data is fake, it may be scaled to mimic the complexity and unpredictability of real-world systems, which increases its utility for these kinds of use cases.

c. **Replicability:** To guarantee consistency in testing, comparable situations and settings can be replicated in an alternative simulated dataset. Models and hypotheses may be tested frequently and improved upon in response to the findings, which makes consistency essential for validation.

2. Benefits of Data Simulation

Data simulation is but one instrument in a company's broader toolkit for managing data. The following are some of the most popular benefits of substituting it for real data, depending on the use cases.

a) Enhanced Decision Making

Decision-making can be aided by data simulation, which models different situations or occurrences and forecasts results depending on actions. This sheds light on speculative situations, enabling the development of appropriate procedures for every case.

b) Cost Efficiency

It is more economical to use data simulation rather than gathered data as it eliminates the requirement for active data collecting and physical testing. Important insights can be gained by simulating various situations and tracking their results without the need for expensive and time-consuming data gathering procedures.

c) Improved Model Validity

Model testing and improvement may be facilitated by data simulation. Building a virtual model of a real-world system allows for the testing of many models and their subsequent improvement depending on the outcomes, resulting in more precise models that are more adept at making detailed predictions about the future.

d) Risk Reduction

Data about crises and possible problems may be obtained via data simulation, which enables organisations to see problems or obstacles before they arise in the actual world. This insight may reduce risks and help you avoid expensive errors.

3. Types of Data Simulation Models

Data simulation models come in a variety of forms, each with special qualities and functionalities. Listed below are the most typical:

a) **Monte Carlo simulations:** This kind of simulation is often used in engineering, science, and finance to model complicated systems and forecast behaviour. It employs random sampling to provide findings for uncertain circumstances.

b) **Agent-based modelling:** It is especially helpful for analysing complex systems because the behaviour of individual components affects the behaviour of the system as a whole. This kind of simulation focusses on the actions and interactions of individual, autonomous agents inside the data systems.

c) **System dynamics:** System dynamics, which is often used in public policy, environmental science, and economics to model and forecast the behaviour of complex systems, aids in the understanding of non-linear feedback loops in increasingly complicated systems.

d) **Discrete-event simulations:** In order to mimic processes and systems, these models—which concentrate on specific system events and their effects on the final result—are often used in computer science, operations research, and logistics.

CHAPTER 5: GENERATIVE AI TECHNIQUES

Learning Objective

This chapter discusses advanced techniques like Variational Autoencoders, GANs, Transformers, and Diffusion Models, showcasing their impact on modern AI applications.

5.1   Variational Autoencoders

Variational autoencoders (VAEs) are generative models that employ deep learning to eliminate noise, identify abnormalities, and create new material.

About the same time as other generative AI algorithms like diffusion models and Generative Adversarial Networks (GANs), VAEs initially appeared in 2013. However, they came before large language models based on the Pathways Language Model, the Generative Pre-trained Transformers (GPT) family, and Bidirectional Encoder Representations from Transformers (BERT).

VAEs are a great option for signal analysis to analyse IoT data streams, biological signals like EEG, or financial data feeds since they are well-suited to creating synthetic time series data that trains other AI algorithms.

VAEs are also appropriate for developing videos, images, and text. However, when creating various types of content,

they are more likely to work in tandem with other models
like transformer models, stable diffusion, which is an
advancement on diffusion models, and GANs.

Similar to GANs, VAEs also integrate two kinds of neural
networks. But VAEs and GANs function in distinct ways.
In the context of VAEs, one network determines more
effective methods to encode unprocessed input into a
latent space, while the second network, known as the
decoder, determines more effective ways to develop new
content from these latent representations. Two neural
networks are used in GANs: one for improved fake
content generation and the other for better fake content
detection.

1. Working of VAEs

All autoencoders are, in general, neural networks that can
learn data. Autoencoders consist of a decoder that
reconstructs the original data from its compressed pieces
and an encoder that breaks up incoming data into smaller
components. An autoencoder, when properly built, will
offer highly accurate decoder output and reconstruct data.
Consequently, the information is acquired in a very
condensed way.

Adding probabilistic features to the encoding process, a
VAE expands upon the fundamentals of an autoencoder.
The word "variational" has been introduced to the
autoencoder lexicon in order to reflect these probabilistic
capabilities. Essentially, a VAE may create a more

extensive data distribution during encoding, and then take a sample from that more extensive data while decoding.

VAEs are able to simulate generations thanks to these additional capabilities. Additionally, it allows VAEs to generate previously unobtainable data, while maintaining the training data set's representativeness.

The four fundamental behaviours listed below help to understand VAEs:

a. The training data teaches the VAE to recognise key components. This is the behaviour of encoding.
b. Using the key components of the training data, the VAE recreates the original data. This is the behaviour of decoding.
c. The VAE may generate various data outputs from the encoded samples by including probabilistic features, such inference, into the encoding side. This mechanism is generative.
d. The VAE efficiently enables VAEs to pursue tasks like unsupervised learning by re-encoding those intricate generative outputs back into a latent space where data is learnt and encoded.

2.   The Architecture of Variational Autoencoder

Variational Autoencoders (VAEs) differ from conventional autoencoders in that they are based on an encoder-decoder design. The encoder network converts unprocessed input data into a latent space probability distribution.

The VAE may describe a range of possible representations rather than simply one point in the latent space since the encoder produces a probabilistic latent code.

A sampled point from the latent distribution is then reconstructed into data space by the decoder network. To reduce the reconstruction loss, or the difference between the input data and the decoded output, the model optimises the encoder and decoder parameters during training. In addition to achieving accurate reconstruction, the objective is to regularise the latent space such that it follows a predetermined distribution.

The reconstruction loss and the regularisation term, which is often represented by the Kullback-Leibler divergence, are two crucial elements that must be carefully balanced throughout the process. Reconstruction loss forces the model to correctly rebuild the input, while regularisation term prevents overfitting and promotes generalisation by encouraging the latent space to follow the selected distribution.

The VAE learns to convert incoming data into a meaningful latent space representation by repeatedly modifying these parameters during training. Accurate reconstruction is made possible by this optimised latent code, which captures the fundamental characteristics and structures of the data. It is also possible to generate new samples by selecting random points from the learnt distribution, thanks to the probabilistic character of the latent space.

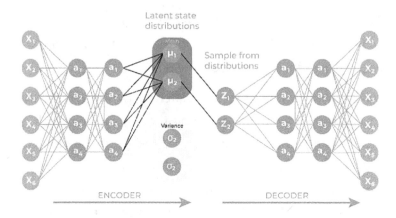

Figure 5.1: VAE architecture. [19]

3. Use of Variational Autoencoders

The three main goals of VAEs are to generate new data, find abnormalities in existing data, and eliminate undesirable or noisy data. Although these three features may not seem remarkable, they enable VAEs to be used in a wide range of potent applications, including the following:

a) **Text creation:** VAEs are able to provide fresh content on a subject in the manner of their choice. Nevertheless, the new text is restricted to the intended style and the training material's scope. For instance, in order to generate a baseball field description in the manner of Mark Twain, the training data set has to include both text that is

---

[19]https://media.geeksforgeeks.org/wp-content/uploads/20231201153426/Variational-AutoEncoder.png

characteristic of Twain's writing and a comprehensive description of baseball fields.

b) **Image creation:** VAEs have the ability to produce new images, but their options are restricted by the training data set. For instance, the training set has to have photos of dogs, poker players, and images that are reflective of Picasso's style in order to produce an image of dogs playing poker in the manner of Picasso.

c) **Video creation:** VAEs can create new video sequences, just as they can create images. The additional video components in this case are also restricted to those found in the training data set.

d) **Language processing:** Complex associations between data pieces may be recognised and comprehended by VAEs. This makes VAEs useful for creating artificial intelligence (AI) entities such as chatbots and digital assistants that can produce speech that sounds both natural and manufactured.

e) **Anomaly detection:** VAEs specialise in time series or sequential data processing and are capable of handling massive amounts of data. Given that the benchmark or typical behaviour of a system has been established, VAEs are thus well suited to anomaly identification in data points.

f) **Synthetic data creation:** VAEs are used by software engineers to create artificial data sets for testing and development. In situations when real-world data is scarce or testing data needs are very high, this streamlines the application development process.

5.2   Generative Adversarial Networks

In 2014, Ian Goodfellow and his colleagues presented Generative Adversarial Networks (GANs). GANs are a kind of neural networks that create new instances that are similar to the original dataset by automatically identifying patterns in the input data.

The Generator and Discriminator neural networks make up the architecture of a GAN. They create synthetic data that is exact replicas of real data via adversarial training.

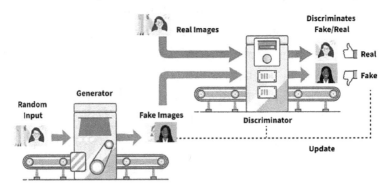

Figure 5.2: Generative Adversarial Networks (GANs). [20]

The two networks play a never-ending game of cat and mouse in which the Generator becomes better at

[20]https://media.geeksforgeeks.org/wp-content/uploads/20250130181755083356/Generative-Adverarial-network-Gans.webp

producing realistic data and the Discriminator gets better at spotting fakes. This adversarial method produces high-quality, realistic data over time.

1. Architecture of GANs

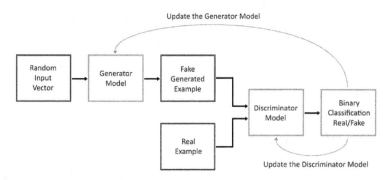

Figure 5.3: Architecture of GANs. [21]

The Generator and the Discriminator neural networks are trained concurrently using adversarial training to form a Generative Adversarial Network (GAN).

a. **Generator**: This network generates data (such as pictures) from random noise. Its objective is to produce data that closely resembles actual data.

b. **Discriminator**: This network endeavours to differentiate between actual data and the data produced by the Generator from its input. It produces the likelihood that the provided data is accurate.

---

[21]https://miro.medium.com/v2/resize:fit:1100/format:webp/1*20e OTTCwC-jGXpbAoc9yVg.png

The Generator attempts to create data during training that the Discriminator is unable to discern from actual data, while the Discriminator seeks to improve its ability to discriminate between genuine and fake data. In essence, the two networks are playing a game of competition: the Generator seeks to create convincingly fictitious data, while the Discriminator seeks to distinguish between genuine and fake. Over time, the Generator produces better and better data as a result of this adversarial process.

2. Types of GANs

GANs can be used for a variety of activities and come in a variety of shapes. The most popular GAN kinds are as follows:

a) **Vanilla GAN:** This is the most basic of all GANs. Using stochastic gradient descent, a technique for learning a whole data set by going over each sample one at a time, its algorithm attempts to optimise the mathematical equation. It is made up of a discriminator and a generator. The discriminator and generator are simple multilayer perceptrons that are used to create and classify produced images. While the generator gathers the data distribution, the discriminator aims to ascertain the probability that the input belongs to a certain class.

b) **Conditional GAN:** This kind of GAN makes it possible to condition the network with novel and targeted information by adding class labels. To assist the network, learn to differentiate between them, the network is given the photos together with their true names, such as "rose," "sunflower," or "tulip," during GAN training.

c) **Deep convolutional GAN:** High-resolution images that can be differentiated are generated by this GAN, which employs a deep convolutional neural network. Convolutions are a method for extracting significant information from the data that is produced. They operate especially effectively with images, allowing the network to swiftly take in the important information.

d) **Self-attention GAN:** This GAN incorporates residually linked self-attention modules, making it a variant of the deep convolutional GAN. This attention-driven architecture is not restricted to spatially local spots; it may build details utilising signals from all feature locations. Consistency between features that are far apart in an image can also be maintained by its discriminator.

e) **CycleGAN:** The most popular GAN architecture, it is often used to learn how to switch between several forms of images. For example, a network may be trained to change a picture from a horse to a zebra or from winter to summer. FaceApp, one of the most well-known uses of CycleGAN, transforms human faces into different age groups.

f) **StyleGAN:** In December 2018, Nvidia researchers published StyleGAN, which suggested major enhancements to the initial generator architecture models. Users have the ability to modify the model to alter the aspect of the images generated by StyleGAN, which is capable of producing photorealistic, high-quality photos of faces. [22]

g) **Super-resolution GAN:** A low-resolution picture may be transformed into a more detailed one using this kind of GAN. Super-resolution GANs fill up areas of blur to improve picture resolution.

h) **Laplacian pyramid GAN:** High picture quality is achieved by this GAN by combining many generator and discriminator networks to create a linear image with band-pass images spaced octave apart, utilising various layers of the Laplacian pyramid.

5.3   Transformers

A neural network architecture known as Transformer is utilised for executing machine learning tasks. In 2017, a paper titled "Attention is all you need" was published by Vaswani and colleagues, introducing the transformers

---

[22]https://www.techtarget.com/searchenterpriseai/definition/gene rative-adversarial-network-GAN#:~:text=Researchers%20from%20Nvidia%20released%20St yleGAN,the%20images%20that%20are%20produced.

architecture. The article examines the design, functionality,
and uses of transformers. [23]

The Transformer Architecture is a model that employs self-
attention to convert an entire sentence into a singular
sentence. This represents a significant change from the
operation of previous models, addressing the difficulties
encountered in architectures such as RNNs and LSTMs.

1. Use Cases for Transformers

Large transformer models can be trained on various types
of sequential data, including human languages, music
compositions, programming languages, and additional
forms. Here are several illustrative use cases.

a) Natural language processing

Machines are now able to understand, interpret, and
generate human language with unprecedented accuracy,
thanks to transformers. Large documents can be
summarised, and coherent, contextually relevant text can
be generated for various use cases. Virtual assistants such
as Alexa utilise transformer technology to comprehend
and react to voice commands.

b) Machine translation

Translation applications utilise transformers to deliver
real-time and precise translations across different

---

[23]https://www.geeksforgeeks.org/getting-started-with-
transformers/

languages. The fluency and accuracy of translations have seen significant improvements with the advent of transformers in comparison to earlier technologies.

c) DNA sequence analysis

By considering segments of DNA as a sequence akin to language, transformers are able to forecast the impacts of genetic mutations, comprehend genetic patterns, and assist in pinpointing areas of DNA linked to specific diseases. This ability is essential for tailored healthcare, as comprehending a person's genetic composition can result in more efficient treatments.

d) Protein structure analysis

Transformer models have the capability to handle sequential data, making them particularly effective for modelling the lengthy sequences of amino acids that fold into intricate protein structures. Grasping the structures of proteins is essential for the discovery of drugs and for comprehending biological processes. Transformers can also be utilised in applications that forecast the 3D structure of proteins derived from their amino acid sequences.

2. Components of Transformer Architecture

The architecture of transformer neural networks consists of multiple software layers that collaborate to produce the final output. The image presented illustrates the components of transformation architecture:

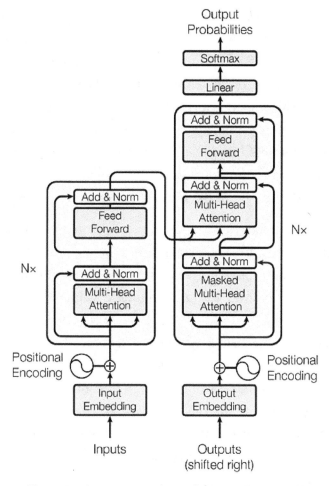

Figure 5.4: Components of transformer architecture. [24]

a) Input Embedding

This phase transforms the input sequence into a mathematical format that is comprehensible to software

---

[24]https://d1.awsstatic.com/GENAI-1.151ded5440b4c997bac0642ec669a00acff2cca1.png

algorithms. The initial step involves dividing the input sequence into a collection of tokens or separate components of the sequence. As an example, when the input consists of a sentence, the tokens represent the words. The embedding process subsequently converts the token sequence into a sequence of mathematical vectors. The vectors hold both semantic and syntactic information, represented numerically, with their characteristics acquired throughout the training process.

Vectors can be visualised as a collection of coordinates within an n-dimensional space. For a straightforward illustration, consider a two-dimensional graph in which the x-axis denotes the alphanumeric value of the initial letter of the word, while the y-axis signifies their respective categories. The term banana holds a value (2,2) as it begins with the letter b and belongs to the category of fruit. The term mango holds a value (13,2) as it begins with the letter m and belongs to the category of fruit. The neural network is therefore informed that the terms "banana" and "mango" belong to the same category via the vector (x,y).

Envision an n-dimensional space where numerous attributes related to the grammar, meaning, and usage of any word are represented by a sequence of numbers. The software is capable of utilising numerical data to compute the relationships among words in mathematical terms, thereby gaining an understanding of the human language model. Embeddings offer a method for representing distinct tokens as continuous vectors that can be processed and learnt from by the model.

b) Positional Encoding

Positional encoding serves as an essential element within the transformer architecture, as the model does not naturally handle sequential data in a specific order. The transformer requires a method to take into account the sequence of the tokens in the input. Positional encoding provides additional information to the embedding of each token, signifying its location within the sequence. This is often accomplished by adding a distinct positional signal to each token's embedding using a collection of functions. The model can comprehend the sequence context and maintain the token order using positional encoding.

c) Transformer Block

A standard transformer model consists of several transformer blocks arranged in a stacked formation. Every transformer block consists of two primary elements: "a multi-head self-attention mechanism and a position-wise feed-forward neural network". The self-attention mechanism allows the model to assess the significance of various tokens in the sequence. The emphasis is placed on pertinent sections of the input during the prediction process.

For example, take into account the phrases "Do not tell lies" and "He lies." The meaning of the word lies in both sentences cannot be grasped without considering the surrounding words. The terms speak and down are crucial for grasping the accurate meaning. The mechanism of self-attention allows for the organisation of pertinent tokens to establish context.

The feed-forward layer includes extra components that enhance the training and functioning efficiency of the transformer model. Each transformer block consists of the following components:

i.   The connections that surround the two primary components function as shortcuts. The flow of information is facilitated from one part of the network to another, bypassing certain operations in between.

ii. Layer normalisation maintains the values—particularly the outputs from various layers within the network—within a specific range to ensure smooth training of the model.

iii. A linear transformation functions to adjust values in a model, enhancing its performance on the specific task for which it is being trained, such as document summarisation rather than translation.

d)   Linear And Softmax Blocks

The model ultimately requires making a specific prediction, like selecting the subsequent word in a sequence. The linear block is introduced at this point. A fully connected layer, often referred to as a dense layer, precedes the final stage. The vector space is mapped to the original input domain using a learnt linear mapping. This essential layer is where the decision-making component of the model transforms the intricate internal representations into specific predictions that are interpretable and usable. This layer produces a collection of scores, commonly referred to as logits, corresponding to each potential token.

The softmax function serves as the concluding step that transforms the logit scores into a normalised probability distribution. Every component of the softmax output indicates the model's level of confidence in a specific class or token.

5.4 Diffusion Models

The natural process of particulate dispersion from high-concentration areas to low-concentration areas until they are uniformly distributed is the inspiration for diffusion models.

Diffusion models, which begin with data and gradually introduce noise to it, use a similar concept in the domain of machine learning. In order to successfully eliminate the noise and reconstruct the data or produce fresh, realistic copies, they subsequently learn to reverse this procedure. This slow conversion produces finely detailed and high-quality outputs that are helpful in applications like autonomous driving, medical imaging, and producing realistic text or graphics.

The distinctive feature of diffusion models is their methodical refining process, which enables them to replicate the natural processes of diffusion and provide very precise and subtle outcomes.

1. Working of Diffusion Models

A neural network is trained to introduce noise into data (the forward diffusion phase) before learning to systematically reverse this process to retrieve the original data or produce new samples. This is how diffusion models function. The following is a descriptive summary of the stages that contribute to the functioning of a diffusion model.

a) Data Preparation:

The data must be properly prepared for training before the diffusion process begins. Cleaning the data to eliminate irregularities, normalising characteristics to preserve consistency, and supplementing the dataset to provide variety—particularly crucial for picture data—are some of the tasks involved in this preparation. A normal distribution is ensured by standardisation, which aids in the efficient management of noisy data. Certain changes, including correcting imbalances in data classes, may be necessary for different kinds of data, like text or images. For the model to receive high-quality input, learn important patterns, and provide realistic outputs while in use, the data must be properly prepared.

b) Forward Diffusion Process:

A basic distribution, usually Gaussian, is used as the starting point for the forward diffusion process. Then, using a Markov chain, this initial sample is gradually changed by a series of reversible stages, each of which adds a little bit more complexity. In order to enable the model to learn and reproduce the complex patterns seen in the target data distribution, structured noise is gradually added when these modifications are implemented. The basic sample will be transformed into one that closely reflects the complexity of the intended data via this procedure. This method shows how starting with basic inputs may lead to outputs that are rich and detailed.

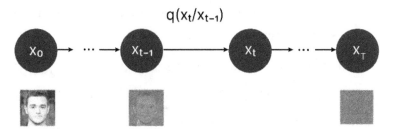

Mathematical formulation:

Let x_0 represent the initial data (e.g., an image). The forward process generates a series of noisy versions of this data $x_1, x_2, \ldots, x_T$ through the following iterative equation:

$$q(x_t \mid x_{t-1}) \sim \mathcal{N}(\sqrt{1 - \beta_t}\, x_{t-1},\ \beta_t I)$$

Here, q is forward process, and x_t is the output of the forward pass at step t. N is a normal distribution, 1-txt-1 is mean, and t_1 defines variance.

c) Reverse Diffusion Process:

The reverse diffusion technique progressively eliminates noise in an attempt to transform pure noise into a clean picture. For a diffusion model to be able to reconstruct an image from pure noise, it must be trained to understand the reverse diffusion process. We're attempting to train our generator network, if you're acquainted with GANs. The main difference is that the diffusion network performs an easier task since it doesn't have to complete everything at once. The writers of this research have determined that it is more effective and easier to train when it employs many processes to eliminate noise at a time.

The mathematical basis for reverse diffusion:

a. **Markov Chain:** A Markov chain model of the diffusion process is used, in which every step is solely dependent on the state that came before it.
b. **Gaussian Noise:** The mean and variance of the noise that is eliminated (and introduced) are usually Gaussian.

The reverse diffusion process aims to reconstruct x_0 from x_T, the noisy data at the final step. This process is modeled by the conditional distribution:

$$p_\theta(\mathbf{x}_{0:T}) = p(\mathbf{x}_T) \prod_{t=1}^{T} p_\theta(\mathbf{x}_{t-1}|\mathbf{x}_t)$$

$$p_\theta(\mathbf{x}_{t-1}|\mathbf{x}_t) = \mathcal{N}(\mathbf{x}_{t-1}; \boldsymbol{\mu}_\theta(\mathbf{x}_t, t), \boldsymbol{\Sigma}_\theta(\mathbf{x}_t, t))$$

Where:

- $\mu\theta(xt,t)$ is the mean predicted by the model,

- $\sigma\theta2(t)$ is the variance, which is usually a function of t and may be learned or predefined.

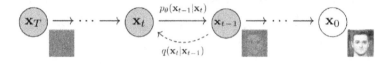

In generative models, the reverse diffusion process is often utilised, as shown in the figure above. The procedure iteratively denoises the picture via time steps T to 0 starting with noise xT. At each step t, a slightly less noisy version xt–1 is predicted from the noisy input xt using a learned model $p_\theta(x_{t-1}|x_t)$.

The dashed arrow labelled $q(x_t|x_{t-1})$ represents the forward diffusion process, while the solid arrow $p_\theta(x_{t-1}|x_t)$ represents the reverse process that is modeled and learned.

5.5 GANs: The Era of Modern Generative AI Begins

At its core, a generative adversarial network consists of two neural networks — a generator and a discriminator — that operate in a continuous feedback loop. The role of the generator is to create new data instances that resemble real-world examples, while the discriminator evaluates the authenticity of these instances. The networks engage in a dynamic competition, in which the generator attempts to produce increasingly credible outputs and the discriminator refines its ability to distinguish between real and generated data. Over time, this adversarial process leads to the production of highly realistic content.

1.   The Evolution and Impact of GANs

Since their inception, GANs have undergone significant evolution. Initially, they were primarily used for generating synthetic images, but researchers soon discovered their vast potential across multiple domains. Some of the most notable applications include:

a)   Image and Video Synthesis

GANs have enabled the creation of photorealistic images, some of which are indistinguishable from actual photographs. Tools like DeepFake technology leverage GANs to manipulate videos, creating seamless and highly believable alterations. In entertainment and media, GANs have been instrumental in special effects, digital character creation, and even restoring old or damaged footage.

b)   Art and Creativity

AI-generated art has become a fascinating field, with GANs producing remarkable pieces that challenge traditional notions of creativity. In 2018, an artwork created by a GAN, titled Portrait of Edmond de Belamy, was auctioned for $432,500, demonstrating the growing intersection between AI and fine art. GANs are also being used in music composition, assisting artists in exploring new creative possibilities.

c) Healthcare and Medicine

The healthcare industry has found promising applications for GANs, particularly in medical imaging and drug discovery. GANs can generate high-resolution medical images to aid in diagnosis, improving the efficiency and accuracy of radiology. Additionally, they are used to simulate molecular structures for pharmaceutical research, expediting the development of new drugs.

d) Gaming and Virtual Reality (VR)

GANs are revolutionising the gaming industry by enhancing the realism of in-game environments and character animations. They are also employed in procedural content generation, where AI dynamically creates game elements based on player interactions. This application extends to virtual reality, where GANs contribute to more immersive and lifelike experiences.

e) Finance and Security

In the financial sector, GANs are used for fraud detection and risk assessment. By generating synthetic financial data, AI models can be trained more effectively to identify anomalies and prevent fraudulent transactions. Additionally, GANs are improving cybersecurity measures by simulating attack scenarios, allowing organisations to strengthen their defence mechanisms.

2. Challenges and Ethical Concerns

While GANs have demonstrated immense potential, they are not without challenges. Some of the key concerns include:

a) Ethical Implications

The ability of GANs to generate realistic deepfakes has sparked ethical debates regarding misinformation and privacy violations. The proliferation of AI-generated fake content poses risks to public trust, journalism, and even political stability.

b) Bias and Fairness

Like other AI models, GANs can inherit biases present in their training data, leading to the generation of biased or misleading outputs. Ensuring fairness in AI-generated content requires rigorous dataset curation and bias mitigation strategies.

c) Computational Costs

GANs require substantial computational power, making them resource-intensive. Training high-quality GANs demands specialised hardware, which can be a barrier for small-scale researchers and enterprises.

d) Legal and Copyright Issues

The rise of AI-generated content raises questions about intellectual property rights. Who owns an artwork created by a GAN? Can an AI-generated song be copyrighted?

These legal ambiguities need to be addressed as AI-generated content becomes more prevalent.

3. The Future of GANs

Despite these challenges, the future of GANs looks promising. Ongoing research aims to refine their efficiency, reduce biases, and develop more ethical AI governance frameworks. Innovations such as progressive growing GANs, self-supervised learning, and hybrid models are expected to enhance their capabilities even further.

As GANs continue to evolve, they are likely to integrate more seamlessly into everyday applications, from personalised digital experiences to AI-powered design and automation. The era of modern generative AI has only just begun, and GANs will undoubtedly play a pivotal role in shaping the technological landscape of the future.

CHAPTER 6: MACHINE LEARNING IN GENERATIVE AI

Learning Objective

This chapter explores how machine learning enhances generative AI by improving model performance, integrating hybrid approaches, and expanding real-world applications. This chapter also explains into innovative techniques for high-quality data generation, enabling more realistic and diverse outputs while addressing various challenges in generative model design and optimisation.

6.1   Enhancing Generative Models

Generative models belong to the broader category of machine learning algorithms that focus on creating new data samples based on patterns observed in training data. Unlike discriminative models, which distinguish between different categories, generative models learn the underlying structure of data and generate new instances that resemble the training data. Enhancing these models requires innovation in architecture design, training strategies, and evaluation metrics.

1.   Architectural Improvements

Improving generative models begins with refining their architectural frameworks. Some various advancements include:

a) Incorporating Attention Mechanisms

Attention mechanisms have significantly boosted the performance of generative models, particularly in text and image generation. By allowing models to focus on specific parts of the input data, they improve coherence and detail in generated outputs. Transformers leverage self-attention mechanisms to capture long-range dependencies, making them highly effective for language generation.

b) Hybrid Model Architectures

Combining different types of generative models can yield superior results. For instance, hybrid models integrating GANs and VAEs leverage the structured latent space of VAEs with the adversarial refinement of GANs, leading to more realistic and diverse outputs. Similarly, diffusion models have been enhanced by incorporating transformer-based architectures for better image generation.

c) Progressive and Hierarchical Generation

Layering generative processes hierarchically allows models to refine details progressively. In image generation, techniques such as StyleGAN utilise a hierarchical approach to control various aspects of an image, from overall structure to fine details. Progressive growing of GANs (ProGANs) also enhances training stability and improves image quality.

2. Training Optimisations

Optimising the training process is critical for enhancing the performance of generative models. Several approaches have been developed to improve convergence, stability, and efficiency.

a) Better Loss Functions

The choice of loss function significantly impacts a generative model's performance. While traditional GANs use binary cross-entropy loss, alternatives such as Wasserstein loss improve training stability by addressing mode collapse. VAEs benefit from the Kullback-Leibler divergence, which ensures structured latent representations.

b) Data Augmentation and Regularisation

Enhancing training data through augmentation techniques helps models generalise better. Data augmentation strategies such as adversarial training, mixup, and contrastive learning refine generative outputs. Regularisation methods, including spectral normalisation and dropout, mitigate overfitting and stabilise training.

c) Efficient Training Strategies

Techniques like curriculum learning, where models start with simpler tasks and gradually move to more complex ones, improve performance. Transfer learning, wherein pre-trained models are fine-tuned on specific datasets, also accelerates training while maintaining high-quality results. Additionally, reinforcement learning has been applied to generative models to refine output quality dynamically.

3. Evaluation and Fine-Tuning

Assessing the quality of generated content is essential for improving generative models. Traditional evaluation metrics such as Mean Squared Error (MSE) often fail to capture the perceptual quality of outputs. More advanced evaluation techniques have emerged, including:

a) Perceptual Metrics

Metrics like the Fréchet Inception Distance (FID) and Inception Score (IS) provide better assessments of generative models by measuring the similarity between generated and real data distributions. Structural Similarity Index (SSIM) is widely used for evaluating image quality.

b) Human Evaluation

Although automated metrics are useful, human judgment remains the gold standard for assessing generated content. Crowdsourced evaluations and expert assessments provide valuable insights into aspects like realism, coherence, and creativity.

c) Iterative Fine-Tuning

Continuous refinement of generative models through fine-tuning on specific datasets enhances their adaptability. Techniques such as reinforcement learning with human feedback (RLHF) enable models to align better with human preferences, improving their utility across diverse applications.

6.2   Hybrid Approaches

Hybrid approaches in machine learning refer to the integration of multiple techniques to optimise performance. In the context of generative AI, these approaches typically combine deep learning with traditional machine learning models or multiple deep learning architectures. The goal is to overcome the limitations of individual techniques and create more robust, adaptable, and generalisable AI models.

Hybrid approaches can be classified into several categories:

a. **Ensemble Learning**: Combining multiple models to improve accuracy.

b. **Neural-Symbolic AI**: Integrating deep learning with symbolic reasoning.

c. **Neuro-Evolutionary Methods**: Using evolutionary algorithms to optimise neural networks.

d. **Multi-Agent Systems**: Deploying multiple AI agents that interact and collaborate.

e. **Transfer Learning and Few-Shot Learning**: Enhancing generative AI by leveraging pre-trained models.

Each of these techniques contributes uniquely to generative AI, enabling it to tackle complex problems with greater efficiency and precision.

1. Ensemble Learning in Generative AI

Ensemble learning is a widely used hybrid approach that combines the predictions of multiple models to enhance overall accuracy and robustness. Techniques such as bagging, boosting, and stacking allow generative AI systems to learn from different perspectives, reducing biases and errors.

For example, in text generation, combining transformer-based models with Recurrent Neural Networks (RNNs) can produce more coherent and contextually aware outputs. In image generation, a mixture of Convolutional Neural Networks (CNNs) and Generative Adversarial Networks (GANs) can improve image sharpness and authenticity. By integrating diverse learning models, ensemble learning enhances the creative potential of generative AI while minimising weaknesses inherent in single-model approaches.

2. Neural-Symbolic AI

Neural-symbolic AI is another hybrid approach that fuses deep learning with symbolic reasoning to improve interpretability and logical consistency. While deep learning excels at pattern recognition and data-driven predictions, symbolic AI offers structured reasoning and explainability.

This approach is particularly beneficial in areas like content generation for legal and medical texts, where logical consistency and factual accuracy are paramount. By incorporating symbolic logic into neural networks, AI systems can better understand relationships between concepts and generate more reliable outputs.

3. Neuro-Evolutionary Methods

Neuro-evolutionary methods apply evolutionary algorithms to optimise neural network architectures, leading to more efficient learning and generalisation. These techniques are useful in generative AI applications where the optimal model structure is unknown or where models need to adapt dynamically to new data.

For instance, evolutionary strategies can fine-tune the architecture of GANs, improving their ability to generate high-fidelity images. This approach also enables adaptive learning in AI-driven music and art generation, where evolving creative styles over time is essential.

4. Multi-Agent Systems in Generative AI

Multi-agent systems involve multiple AI entities that interact and collaborate to achieve complex generative tasks. In the context of generative AI, this approach can be used to create more dynamic and responsive AI models.

For example, in game development, AI agents can generate interactive storylines by adapting to user choices in real time. Similarly, in conversational AI, multiple chatbot models can work together to create more engaging and meaningful dialogues. The collaborative nature of multi-agent systems enables generative AI to handle diverse scenarios more effectively.

148

5.   Transfer Learning and Few-Shot Learning

Transfer learning and few-shot learning are hybrid
strategies that leverage pre-trained models to generate
high-quality outputs with limited data. Instead of training
a generative model from scratch, AI systems can build
upon existing knowledge, reducing computational
requirements and improving efficiency.

This approach is particularly valuable in domains where
labelled data is scarce, such as medical image synthesis
and personalised content generation. By fine-tuning pre-
trained models on domain-specific data, generative AI can
achieve high levels of accuracy even with minimal training
examples.

6.3   Applications

Generative AI refers to systems that can create new data,
whether in the form of text, images, audio, or even code,
often with remarkable accuracy and coherence. Machine
learning plays a crucial role in enabling these capabilities,
providing the foundation upon which generative models
are built.

1.   Natural Language Processing (NLP) and Text
Generation

One of the most prominent applications of generative AI
powered by machine learning is natural language
processing (NLP). Models such as OpenAI's GPT series
and Google's BERT have revolutionised text-based
interactions by generating coherent and contextually

relevant text. These advancements have led to numerous applications, including:

  a. **Chatbots and Virtual Assistants**: AI-powered chatbots and virtual assistants utilise machine learning to understand and generate human-like responses, enhancing customer service and user engagement.

  b. **Content Creation**: Machine learning models can generate articles, reports, and even poetry, assisting writers by providing suggestions or creating drafts based on given prompts.

  c. **Language Translation**: Neural machine translation (NMT) models improve upon traditional rule-based translation methods, producing more natural and accurate translations across different languages.

  d. **Summarisation and Paraphrasing**: AI-driven summarisation tools help condense large volumes of text into concise summaries, making information more digestible for users.

2. Image Generation and Enhancement

Generative AI has made remarkable strides in image synthesis and enhancement, primarily through deep learning techniques such as generative adversarial networks (GANs) and variational autoencoders (VAEs). These advancements have led to practical applications in multiple fields:

a. **Art and Design**: AI-driven tools like DeepArt and
   DALL·E allow artists and designers to generate
   unique digital artwork based on textual prompts or
   stylistic inputs.

b. **Photography and Image Editing**: Machine learning
   models can enhance image quality, remove noise,
   upscale resolution, and even colourise black-and-
   white images.

c. **Synthetic Media**: AI-generated faces and
   landscapes have applications in marketing,
   gaming, and filmmaking, reducing the need for
   traditional photoshoots.

d. **Medical Imaging**: Machine learning algorithms
   improve diagnostic accuracy by generating clearer
   medical scans, assisting healthcare professionals in
   detecting anomalies.

3. **Audio and Music Generation**

Machine learning has also revolutionised the creation and
manipulation of audio content. Generative AI can
synthesise human-like speech, compose original music,
and enhance audio quality. Key applications include:

a. **Speech Synthesis and Voice Cloning**: AI-driven
   text-to-speech (TTS) models generate natural-
   sounding voices, improving accessibility for
   visually impaired individuals and enabling realistic
   voiceovers.

b. **Music Composition**: AI models like OpenAI's
   MuseNet and Google's Magenta can generate

melodies, harmonies, and full compositions based on predefined styles and user inputs.

c. **Audio Restoration**: Machine learning algorithms help restore old or damaged recordings by removing noise, enhancing clarity, and filling in missing sections.

d. **Podcast and Audiobook Narration**: Generative AI can create realistic voice narrations, reducing the reliance on human voice actors while maintaining high-quality storytelling.

4. Video Creation and Deepfake Technology

Generative AI has significantly impacted video production, enabling the creation of realistic videos and animations. While deepfake technology has raised ethical concerns, it has also provided valuable applications:

a. **Film and Media Industry**: AI-generated characters and scenes reduce production costs and enhance visual effects in movies and video games.

b. **Virtual Influencers**: Brands use AI-generated personas to interact with audiences, reducing reliance on human influencers while maintaining engagement.

c. **Synthetic Training Data**: AI-generated videos help train autonomous systems, such as self-driving cars, by simulating real-world scenarios.

d. **Forensic and Security Applications**: Machine learning can detect deepfake content, aiding in the prevention of misinformation and identity fraud.

5. Code Generation and Software Development

Machine learning-powered generative AI has revolutionised software development by automating code generation and optimisation. Developers can leverage AI tools to enhance productivity and reduce manual effort. Various applications include:

a. **Automated Code Completion**: AI models, such as GitHub Copilot and OpenAI Codex, assist developers by suggesting code snippets and completing functions.

b. **Bug Detection and Fixing**: Machine learning algorithms identify potential bugs and vulnerabilities in code, improving software reliability.

c. **Low-Code/No-Code Development**: AI-powered platforms enable non-programmers to create software applications using simple drag-and-drop interfaces.

d. **Algorithm Optimisation**: AI enhances software performance by optimising code structures and improving execution efficiency.

6. Drug Discovery and Scientific Research

In the healthcare and scientific research sectors, machine learning in generative AI is accelerating discoveries and innovations. AI-driven models are assisting researchers in generating new hypotheses, simulating experiments, and uncovering novel solutions. Applications include:

a. **Drug Discovery**: AI-generated molecular structures help pharmaceutical companies identify potential drug candidates more efficiently.

b. **Genetic Research**: Machine learning algorithms analyse DNA sequences, aiding in disease prediction and personalised medicine.

c. **Material Science**: AI models generate new materials with desirable properties for use in construction, electronics, and medical applications.

d. **Climate Modelling**: AI-driven simulations help scientists predict climate changes and develop strategies for environmental sustainability.

7. **Game Development and Virtual Worlds**

Generative AI is transforming the gaming industry by automating the creation of realistic environments, characters, and narratives. Machine learning enables dynamic content generation, enhancing player experiences. Applications include:

a. **Procedural Content Generation**: AI creates diverse landscapes, levels, and missions, reducing development time and enhancing replay-ability.

b. **NPC Behaviour Modelling**: Machine learning enhances non-playable characters (NPCs), making them more intelligent and responsive.

c. **Adaptive Storytelling**: AI-driven narratives adjust to player choices, creating immersive and personalised gaming experiences.

    **d. Virtual Reality (VR) and Augmented Reality
(AR)**: AI-generated content enhances interactive
and immersive virtual experiences.

6.4   Innovative Approaches for High-Quality Data Generation

In today's digital age, the importance of high-quality data
cannot be overstated. Accurate and reliable data is the
cornerstone of informed decision-making across
industries, from healthcare and finance to marketing and
artificial intelligence. However, generating high-quality
data presents numerous challenges, including issues of
bias, inconsistencies, and incompleteness.

1. Leveraging Artificial Intelligence and Machine Learning

Artificial intelligence (AI) and machine learning (ML) have
revolutionised data generation by enabling automated,
intelligent data collection and validation processes. AI-
powered algorithms can analyse vast amounts of data,
identify patterns, and eliminate inconsistencies, ensuring
high data quality. Machine learning models can also
generate synthetic data—artificially created data that
mimics real-world datasets—providing a viable solution
for industries where real data is scarce or sensitive.

One prominent example is the use of generative
adversarial networks (GANs), which create synthetic
datasets for training AI models in healthcare, finance, and
autonomous driving. By simulating real-world conditions,

GANs ensure that models are trained on diverse, high-quality data, reducing bias and improving accuracy.

2. Blockchain Technology for Data Integrity

Blockchain technology offers a decentralised and tamper-proof approach to data generation and storage. By using cryptographic security and distributed ledger systems, blockchain ensures data integrity, transparency, and trustworthiness. This technology is particularly valuable in industries such as supply chain management, healthcare, and finance, where data security is paramount.

For instance, blockchain is used to verify transactions in financial institutions, preventing fraud and ensuring compliance with regulatory standards. In healthcare, patient records stored on blockchain networks maintain accuracy while allowing secure access for authorised users.

3. Crowdsourcing and Human-in-the-Loop Systems

Crowdsourcing has emerged as a powerful method for generating high-quality data. By leveraging the collective intelligence of diverse contributors, organisations can obtain large volumes of data with improved accuracy and reliability. Platforms like Amazon Mechanical Turk enable businesses to gather and validate data through human participation.

Human-In-The-Loop (HITL) systems combine human intelligence with automated processes to refine data quality further. In these systems, human experts oversee

data labelling, validation, and quality control, ensuring
that AI-generated data remains accurate and unbiased.

4. IoT and Sensor-Based Data Collection

The Internet of Things (IoT) has transformed data
generation through real-time sensor-based data collection.
IoT devices, including smart meters, wearables, and
industrial sensors, continuously capture and transmit data,
providing real-time insights across various sectors.

For example, in agriculture, IoT-enabled sensors monitor
soil moisture levels, weather conditions, and crop health,
allowing farmers to make data-driven decisions that
enhance productivity. Similarly, in smart cities, IoT sensors
collect traffic and environmental data to optimise urban
planning and infrastructure development.

5. Data Augmentation and Preprocessing Techniques

Data augmentation enhances the quality of existing
datasets by generating additional variations, reducing
biases, and improving model generalisation. This
technique is widely used in machine learning applications,
particularly in image and speech recognition.

Additionally, preprocessing techniques such as data
normalisation, deduplication, and outlier detection play a
crucial role in improving data quality. Normalisation
ensures consistency in data formats, while deduplication
removes redundant information. Outlier detection
identifies and addresses anomalies, preventing
inaccuracies from distorting analyses.

6. Privacy-Preserving Data Generation

As data privacy concerns continue to rise, innovative privacy-preserving techniques have gained traction. Differential privacy and federated learning are two notable approaches that enable data sharing without compromising individual privacy.

Differential privacy adds controlled noise to datasets, allowing organisations to analyse trends without exposing sensitive information. Federated learning, on the other hand, enables AI models to be trained across multiple devices without transferring raw data, preserving user privacy while improving data accuracy.

7. Synthetic Data for Training AI Models

Synthetic data has become an invaluable resource for AI model training, particularly in scenarios where real-world data is limited, expensive, or sensitive. By generating artificial datasets that closely resemble real data, businesses can train machine learning models effectively without the risks associated with data privacy and bias.

For instance, in healthcare, synthetic patient data is used to develop predictive models without violating patient confidentiality. In the financial sector, synthetic transaction data helps in fraud detection model training while ensuring regulatory compliance.

8. Edge Computing for Real-Time Data Processing

Edge computing has emerged as a game-changer in high-quality data generation by enabling real-time processing at the data source. Unlike traditional cloud computing, where data is sent to centralised servers, edge computing processes data closer to its origin, reducing latency and improving accuracy.

This approach is particularly beneficial in applications such as autonomous vehicles, where real-time decision-making is crucial. By processing data locally on edge devices, self-driving cars can react faster to environmental changes, enhancing safety and performance.

9. Reinforcement Learning for Data Optimisation

Reinforcement learning (RL) is increasingly being used to optimise data generation processes. RL algorithms learn from interactions with the environment, continuously refining their data collection strategies to maximise accuracy and efficiency.

A notable application is in customer service chatbots, where RL models learn from user interactions to generate more relevant and context-aware responses over time. Similarly, in financial risk assessment, RL techniques help refine predictive models by iteratively improving data selection and analysis.

10. Automated Data Pipelines and Cloud-Based Solutions

The adoption of automated data pipelines and cloud-based solutions has streamlined high-quality data generation for businesses. Automated pipelines facilitate seamless data ingestion, transformation, and validation, reducing manual errors and ensuring consistency.

Cloud-based platforms, such as Google Cloud, AWS, and Microsoft Azure, offer scalable and secure data storage and processing solutions. These platforms integrate AI-driven tools for data cleansing, enrichment, and analytics, enabling organisations to maintain high-quality datasets efficiently.

CHAPTER 7: DEEP LEARNING IN GENERATIVE AI

Learning Objective

This chapter examines the role of deep learning architectures in generative AI, focusing on Convolutional and Recurrent Neural Networks, deep generative models, and training challenges. It further explores AI's evolution in generating realistic images and text, highlighting breakthroughs and challenges in deep learning-driven generative AI.

7.1 Convolutional Neural Networks

A Convolutional Neural Network (CNN) represents an advanced form of artificial neural networks (ANN) primarily utilised for feature extraction from grid-like matrix datasets. For instance, visual datasets such as images or videos, in which data patterns have a significant impact.

1. CNN Architecture

A Convolutional Neural Network is composed of several layers, including "the input layer, convolutional layer, pooling layer, and fully connected layers".

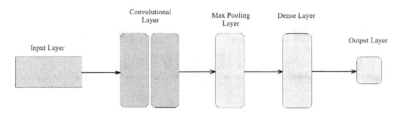

Figure 7.1: Simple CNN architecture. [25]

The Convolutional layer utilises filters on the input image to extract features, while the Pooling layer reduces the image size to decrease computation, and the fully connected layer produces the final prediction. The network acquires the best filters by utilising backpropagation and gradient descent techniques.

2. Working of Convolutional Layers

Convolutional Neural Networks, often referred to as covnets, are a type of neural network that utilises shared parameters. Consider having a picture. A cuboid can represent it, characterised by its length, width (the dimensions of the image), and height (referring to the channels, as images typically consist of red, green, and blue channels).

---

[25]https://ars.els-cdn.com/content/image/1-s2.0-S0306261924005130-gr4_lrg.jpg

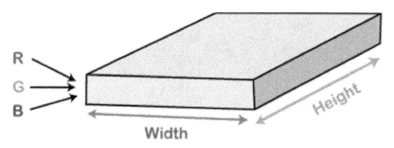

Figure 7.2: A cuboid having length, width, and height. [26]

Now envision extracting a small section of this image and applying a small neural network, referred to as a filter or kernel, to it, producing K outputs that are arranged vertically. The neural network is then slid across the entire image, resulting in a new image that features varying widths, heights, and depths. Now, there are additional channels available, though the width and height have been reduced compared to just R, G, and B channels. The operation is referred to as Convolution. If the patch size matches the dimensions of the image, it will function as a conventional neural network. The presence of this small patch results in a reduction of weights.

---

[26]https://encrypted-tbn3.gstatic.com/images?q=tbn:ANd9GcQkh9AjLLhxGkH3_YInv_9bXgxnfF4Tr8bn23-n20-7BnOcYmqA

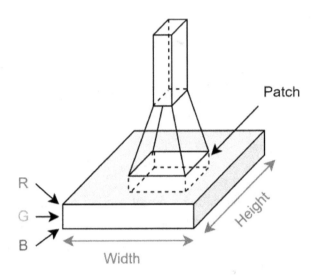

R

G →

B

Width

Figure 7.3: Deep Learning Udacity. [27]

3. Mathematical Overview of Convolution

Some mathematical concepts that are part of the convolution process:

a. Convolution layers are made up of a collection of learnable filters, also known as kernels, which possess small widths and heights while maintaining the same depth as the input volume, typically three if the input layer is an image.

b. For instance, when performing convolution on an image that measures 34x34x3. The potential dimensions of filters can be represented as axax3,

---

[27]https://ars.els-cdn.com/content/image/1-s2.0-S152614922400050X-CMES_50760-fig-3.gif

with 'a' being any value such as 3, 5, or 7, provided it is smaller than the dimensions of the image.

c. In the forward pass, each filter is slid across the entire input volume incrementally, with each increment referred to as stride, which may take values of 2, 3, or even 4 for high-dimensional images. The dot product is then calculated between the kernel weights and the corresponding patch from the input volume.

d. By sliding the filters, a 2-D output will be generated for each filter, and when these outputs are stacked together, the resulting output volume will have a depth that corresponds to the number of filters used. The network is set to learn all the filters.

7.2   Recurrent Neural Networks

Recurrent neural networks are a variety of neural network that is both potent and robust. They are among the most promising algorithms currently in use due to the fact that they are the only sort of neural network that has an internal memory.

RNNs are very accurate in anticipating future events because they are able to retain significant details about the input they have received. For sequential data such as time series, voice, text, financial data, audio, video, weather, and much more, this is the reason they are the algorithm of choice. Compared to other algorithms, recurrent neural networks are able to develop a much deeper grasp of a sequence and its context.

1. Working of Recurrent Neural Network

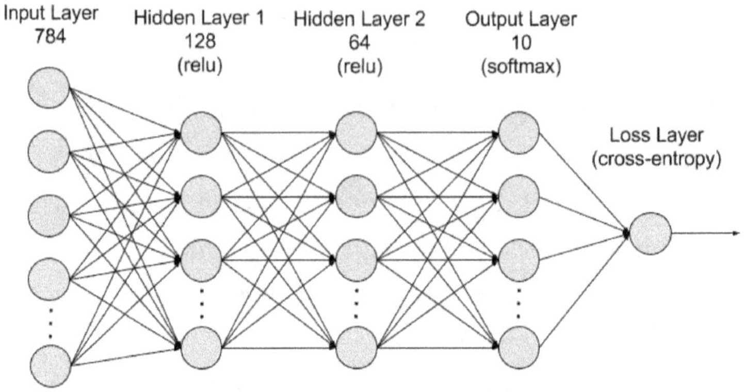

Figure 7.4: Diagram of an RNN. [28]

Neurons, which are data-processing nodes that collaborate to carry out intricate tasks, make up RNNs. Input, output, and hidden layers make up the arrangement of the neurons. The output layer delivers the outcome after the input layer gets the data to process. The hidden layer is where data processing, analysis, and prediction occurs.

a) Hidden Layer

One step at a time, RNNs receive sequential data which they transmit to hidden layers. But they also have a recurring or self-looping workflow: a short-term memory component allows the hidden layer to remember and use previous inputs for predictions in the future. To predict a

---

[28]https://d2908q01vomqb2.cloudfront.net/f1f836cb4ea6efb2a0b1b99f41ad8b103eff4b59/2017/10/06/intro-gluon-1.gif

subsequent sequence, it uses both the stored memory and the current input.

For example, consider the following sequence: Apple is red. Red is the colour the RNN wants to predict when it receives the input sequence Apple is. A duplicate of the word Apple is stored in the hidden layer's memory once it has been processed. It then recognizes Apple from memory when it encounters the word is and understands the entire sequence: Apple is for context. Then, for increased accuracy, it can predict red. Because of this, RNNs are helpful for language modelling applications such as machine translation and audio recognition.

b) Training

In order to train deep neural networks, such as RNNs, machine learning (ML) engineers feed the model training data and improve its performance. In machine learning, the weights of the neurones serve as signals that indicate how much the information acquired during training influences the output prediction. An RNN's layers all have the same weight.

To increase the accuracy of predictions, machine learning engineers modify weights. They compute model error and modify its weight based on it using a method known as backpropagation through time (BPTT). BPTT recalculates the error rate and rolls back the output to the prior time step. It may then alter the weight to lower the error margin and determine which hidden state in the sequence is generating a substantial inaccuracy.

2. Types of Recurrent Neural Networks

RNNs can be divided into four categories according on the network's input and output numbers:

a) One-to-One RNN

There is just one input and one output in this kind of neural network design, which is the most basic. It is used for simple classification jobs that don't need sequential data, such binary classification.

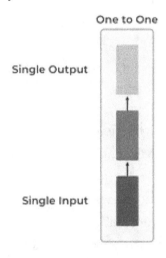

Figure 7.5: One to One RNN. [29]

b) One-to-Many RNN

Over time, a One-to-Many RNN generates several outputs by processing a single input. When one input sets off a

---

[29]https://media.geeksforgeeks.org/wp-content/uploads/20231204131135/One-to-One-300.webp

series of predictions (outputs), this is helpful. For instance, in image captioning, a single image can be utilised as input to produce a string of words that will be used as the caption.

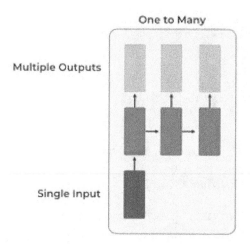

Figure 7.6: One-to-Many RNN. [30]

c) Many-to-One RNN

The Many-to-One RNN produces a single output after receiving a series of inputs. When a single prediction requires knowledge of the input sequence's general context, this type is helpful. When a phrase or other string of words is fed into a sentiment analysis model, it generates a single output that may be classified as positive, negative, or neutral.

---

[30]https://media.geeksforgeeks.org/wp-content/uploads/20231204131304/One-to-Many-300.webp

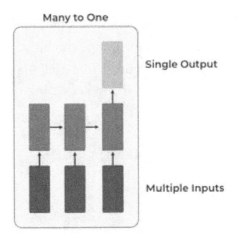

Figure 7.7: Many-to-One RNN. [31]

d) Many-to-Many RNN

A series of inputs is processed by the Many-to-Many RNN type, which then produces a sequence of outputs. A set of words in one language is provided as input in a language translation process, and the output is a matching set of words in another language.

---

[31]https://media.geeksforgeeks.org/wp-content/uploads/20231204131355/Many-to-One-300.webp

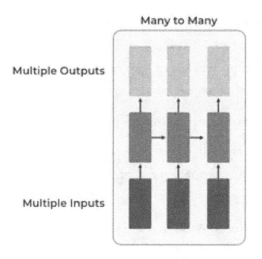

Figure 7.8: Many-to-Many RNN. [32]

7.3   Deep Generative Models

Deep generative models are a class of neural networks trained to generate new data samples similar to those in their training dataset. They achieve this by learning the probability distribution of the input data and sampling from it to create new instances. These models leverage deep learning techniques, particularly neural networks, to capture complex patterns and relationships within the data.

Generative models contrast with discriminative models, which focus on distinguishing between different data categories. While discriminative models, such as

---

[32]https://media.geeksforgeeks.org/wp-content/uploads/20231204131436/Many-to-Many-300.webp

convolutional neural networks (CNNs) and recurrent neural networks (RNNs), are trained to classify inputs, generative models attempt to reconstruct or generate novel instances from learned distributions.

1. Types of Deep Generative Models

There are several types of deep generative models, each with unique approaches and applications. The most notable ones include:

a) Variational Autoencoders (VAEs)

VAEs are probabilistic models that use encoder-decoder architectures to generate new data samples. The encoder compresses the input data into a lower-dimensional latent space, while the decoder reconstructs it back to the original form. By introducing a probabilistic layer, VAEs ensure smooth sampling, enabling the generation of diverse outputs. These models are widely used in image synthesis, anomaly detection, and data augmentation.

b) Generative Adversarial Networks (GANs)

GANs consist of two neural networks, a generator and a discriminator, engaged in a competitive process. The generator creates synthetic data, while the discriminator evaluates its authenticity. Through this adversarial training, GANs refine their ability to produce realistic samples. They have gained popularity in generating high-resolution images, deepfake videos, and even realistic human speech.

c) Normalising Flows

Normalising flow models use invertible transformations to map a simple probability distribution (such as a Gaussian distribution) into a more complex one that resembles the target data distribution. These models are highly effective in density estimation and data synthesis, offering advantages in interpretability and sampling efficiency.

d) Autoregressive Models

Autoregressive models generate data sequentially, predicting the next value based on previously generated values. Popular examples include PixelCNN and WaveNet, which are used for image and audio generation, respectively. These models offer high-quality outputs but are often computationally expensive due to their sequential nature.

2. Applications of Deep Generative Models

The ability of deep generative models to create realistic and diverse data has led to their adoption across multiple domains. Some of the most impactful applications include:

a) Image Generation and Enhancement

Generative models are extensively used in computer vision for image synthesis, super-resolution, and style transfer. GANs, in particular, have enabled the creation of photorealistic images and artwork that mimic human creativity.

b) Text Generation and Language Modelling

Natural Language Processing (NLP) has benefited immensely from generative models, especially in applications like automated content creation, chatbots, and machine translation. Models like GPT (Generative Pre-trained Transformer) leverage autoregressive methods to generate coherent and contextually relevant text.

c) Drug Discovery and Medical Research

In healthcare, generative models aid in drug discovery by simulating molecular structures and predicting their properties. This accelerates the development of new medicines and enhances personalised treatment plans.

d) Music and Audio Synthesis

AI-generated music has become a reality with the advancement of generative models. WaveNet and similar architectures produce highly realistic speech and music, enabling applications in virtual assistants, audiobooks, and music composition.

e) Video Game Development and Virtual Worlds

Generative models contribute to video game design by creating realistic textures, landscapes, and character animations. This significantly reduces the workload of human designers while maintaining high-quality visual elements.

3. Advantages of Deep Generative Models

Deep generative models offer numerous advantages that
make them indispensable in modern AI applications:

a. **Data Augmentation:** They generate synthetic data
   to improve machine learning models, especially
   when labelled data is scarce.

b. **High-Quality Output:** Advanced generative
   models produce highly realistic images, text, and
   audio that often surpass human-created content.

c. **Unsupervised Learning:** Unlike traditional
   supervised learning models, generative models can
   learn from unlabelled data, making them useful in
   scenarios where labelling is expensive or
   impractical.

d. **Creativity and Innovation:** They enable AI systems
   to generate novel and unique content, fostering
   innovation in creative industries such as art, music,
   and design.

7.4   Training Challenges

Models such as GPT-4, DALL-E, and Stable Diffusion
demonstrate the potential of AI in generating text, images,
music, and even code with remarkable sophistication.
However, training these generative AI models presents
significant challenges that researchers and developers
must navigate. Understanding these challenges is crucial
for advancing AI capabilities while ensuring ethical,
scalable, and efficient development.

1. Data Quality and Availability

One of the fundamental challenges in training generative AI is acquiring high-quality and diverse datasets. AI models require vast amounts of data to learn patterns and generate coherent outputs. However, sourcing data that is representative, unbiased, and ethically obtained is a major hurdle.

   a. **Bias in Data**: Many datasets contain inherent biases, leading to skewed AI outputs that may reinforce stereotypes or misinformation.
   b. **Copyright Issues**: Using copyrighted material for training raises legal and ethical concerns, prompting researchers to seek open-source or proprietary datasets.
   c. **Data Scarcity**: For niche domains, such as medical or legal AI, high-quality data is often limited and expensive.

Addressing these issues requires developing synthetic datasets, improving data curation processes, and implementing strict data governance policies.

2. Computational Costs and Infrastructure

Training generative AI models demands extensive computational resources, making it both costly and energy-intensive.

   a. **High Hardware Requirements**: Training state-of-the-art models necessitates powerful GPUs or

TPUs, which are expensive and have limited availability.

b. **Energy Consumption**: AI training consumes vast amounts of electricity, raising concerns about environmental sustainability.

c. **Cloud vs. On-Premise Training**: Organisations must decide whether to train models in-house or use cloud-based solutions, balancing cost and control.

Efforts to optimise AI training, such as efficient model architectures and energy-efficient hardware, are essential to mitigating these challenges.

3. Model Complexity and Training Stability

Generative AI models, particularly deep learning architectures like transformers, are highly complex, making them challenging to train and fine-tune.

a. **Vanishing and Exploding Gradients**: Training deep neural networks can suffer from unstable gradient updates, causing convergence issues.

b. **Hyperparameter Tuning**: Selecting appropriate learning rates, batch sizes, and other hyperparameters requires extensive experimentation.

c. **Mode Collapse**: In generative adversarial networks (GANs), mode collapse occurs when the generator produces limited variations, reducing creativity.

Researchers employ techniques like adaptive learning rates, gradient clipping, and advanced regularisation methods to address these issues.

4. Ethical and Bias Concerns

Ethical considerations in generative AI are paramount, as biased or inappropriate outputs can have far-reaching consequences.

a. **Misinformation and Deepfakes**: Generative AI can be misused to create deepfake videos or generate misleading information.

b. **Bias and Fairness**: AI models trained on biased datasets can perpetuate discrimination, making fairness and inclusivity key concerns.

c. **Transparency and Accountability**: AI-generated content often lacks explainability, raising questions about accountability in decision-making.

Addressing these concerns involves implementing bias mitigation techniques, promoting transparency in AI decision-making, and enforcing ethical AI guidelines.

5. Training Data Security and Privacy

The use of large-scale datasets, especially those containing personal information, raises serious security and privacy concerns.

a. **Data Anonymisation**: Ensuring that personally identifiable information (PII) is removed from training data.

b. **Secure Model Training**: Protecting AI models from adversarial attacks that manipulate training data.

c. **Compliance with Regulations**: Adhering to global data protection laws, such as GDPR and India's Data Protection Bill.

Secure federated learning and differential privacy techniques are being explored to enhance data security in AI training.

6. Generalisation and Robustness

Generative AI models must generalise well to diverse scenarios without overfitting to training data.

a. **Overfitting vs. Underfitting**: Striking a balance between model complexity and generalisation is a persistent challenge.

b. **Handling Noisy Data**: Real-world datasets often contain errors, requiring robust data-cleaning methods.

c. **Transfer Learning Limitations**: While transfer learning can enhance model efficiency, it may not always generalise effectively across domains.

Research into improved loss functions, data augmentation, and adversarial training aims to enhance model robustness.

7. Human-AI Interaction and Usability

For generative AI to be widely adopted, models must be user-friendly and adaptable to human needs.

a. **Interpretability**: Understanding how AI models generate specific outputs remains a challenge.

b. **Fine-tuning for Specific Use Cases**: Customising generative models for particular industries requires extensive fine-tuning.

c. **Human-in-the-Loop Approaches**: Incorporating human oversight in AI-generated content ensures higher quality and ethical alignment.

Developing intuitive AI interfaces and interactive training methods will enhance the usability of generative AI models.

7.5 From Pixels to Perfection: The Evolution of AI Image Generation

Among the most remarkable developments is AI-powered image generation, an area that has witnessed extraordinary progress over the past few decades. What once seemed like science fiction—computers generating realistic, high-quality images—has now become a reality. This evolution, from rudimentary pixel-based outputs to near-perfect, hyper-realistic imagery, highlights the power of AI in reshaping visual creativity.

1. Early Days - The Foundations of Computer Graphics

Before AI played a role in image creation, computer graphics were dominated by algorithmic and rule-based approaches. In the 1960s and 70s, pioneers in computer graphics developed basic image-rendering techniques, relying on mathematical formulas and structured data to generate visuals. The introduction of raster graphics allowed computers to process images as collections of pixels, laying the groundwork for digital artistry.

The 1980s and 90s saw the rise of Computer-Generated Imagery (CGI) in film and gaming. However, these images required extensive manual input and computational effort, limiting their accessibility and flexibility. While CGI could produce stunning visuals, the process was painstakingly slow and lacked the dynamic adaptability that AI would later introduce.

2. The Emergence of AI in Image Processing

The integration of AI into image generation began with neural networks and deep learning. By the early 2000s, machine learning algorithms enabled computers to recognise patterns in images, enhancing image classification and basic enhancements. Convolutional Neural Networks (CNNs), a major breakthrough in deep learning, enabled more sophisticated image processing, paving the way for AI-driven creativity.

A significant milestone came with the introduction of Generative Adversarial Networks (GANs) in 2014 by Ian Goodfellow and his team. GANs revolutionised AI-generated imagery by using two neural networks—a generator and a discriminator—competing against each other to produce increasingly realistic images. This adversarial training process allowed AI to generate faces, landscapes, and even artworks that were indistinguishable from those created by human artists.

3. The Rise of Deep Learning and Neural Networks

Following GANs, deep learning techniques such as Variational Autoencoders (VAEs) and Transformers further enhanced AI image generation. VAEs improved the quality of generated images by refining the probability distributions of pixels, resulting in smoother, more detailed outputs. Meanwhile, diffusion models, an advanced AI technique, have recently gained traction for their ability to generate stunningly realistic images by gradually refining noise-based inputs into coherent visuals.

With AI models like DALL-E, Midjourney, and Stable Diffusion, image generation has reached new heights. These AI systems are capable of generating complex and highly detailed images from textual prompts, democratising digital artistry by making high-quality visuals accessible to a broader audience.

4. AI Image Generation in Art and Media

The impact of AI-generated imagery extends beyond mere novelty; it is reshaping the creative industries. Artists and designers now use AI as a tool to augment their creativity, generating ideas, refining concepts, and producing intricate visuals that would otherwise require extensive manual effort.

In media and entertainment, AI-generated images are revolutionising content creation. From generating virtual characters to producing synthetic stock images, AI is reducing costs and enhancing efficiency. Advertisers and marketers leverage AI-generated visuals to create tailored campaigns, while filmmakers explore AI-generated backgrounds and special effects to streamline production processes.

5. Ethical and Legal Considerations

Despite its advantages, AI image generation raises ethical and legal concerns. One major issue is the potential for deepfakes—hyper-realistic AI-generated images and videos used to spread misinformation. The ease with which AI can generate convincing fake visuals has sparked debates about digital ethics and media credibility.

Moreover, the question of intellectual property remains unresolved. When an AI generates an image based on millions of pre-existing artworks, who owns the rights to the final output? Many artists have raised concerns about AI models trained on their work without permission, leading to discussions about copyright laws and fair use policies in the digital era.

6. The Future of AI Image Generation

As AI continues to evolve, the future of image generation promises even greater advancements. Real-time AI image synthesis could revolutionise gaming, allowing for dynamic and interactive visual storytelling. Additionally, AI-powered tools will likely become more refined, assisting professionals across various industries, from fashion and architecture to healthcare and forensic science.

One potential development is the integration of AI image generation with augmented reality (AR) and virtual reality (VR), creating immersive digital experiences that blur the lines between the real and the artificial. Furthermore, improvements in AI ethics and regulation will be crucial to ensuring responsible use of this technology, balancing innovation with accountability.

7.6   Tech Triumphs in Text Generation

The ability of AI to generate human-like text has transformed sectors such as journalism, marketing, customer service, and even creative writing. These technological triumphs are not just about automation but also about the nuanced understanding of language, context, and creativity.

1.   The Evolution of Text Generation Technology

Text generation has undergone a significant transformation over the past few decades. From simple rule-based systems that could only generate structured, repetitive text to sophisticated neural networks that produce coherent and context-aware content, the progress has been extraordinary.

One of the earliest forms of text generation relied on predefined templates and rule-based algorithms. These systems were rigid and lacked the ability to adapt to varying contexts. With the advent of machine learning, particularly natural language processing (NLP), text generation saw a significant shift. Models like OpenAI's

GPT series and Google's BERT introduced deep learning architectures capable of understanding context, syntax, and semantics at an advanced level.

The introduction of transformers, a type of neural network architecture, was a turning point in AI-driven text generation. Unlike previous models, transformers use self-attention mechanisms to weigh the importance of different words in a sentence, allowing them to generate more coherent and contextually relevant text. This has made AI-generated content increasingly indistinguishable from human-written text.

2. Breakthroughs in Text Generation

Several innovations have contributed to the success of AI-driven text generation:

a) Large-Scale Pretrained Models

Large language models such as GPT-4 and LLaMA-2 have demonstrated exceptional proficiency in generating human-like text. These models are trained on massive datasets, enabling them to understand a wide array of topics and writing styles. Their ability to generate contextually appropriate and grammatically accurate text has redefined how businesses approach content creation.

b) Few-Shot and Zero-Shot Learning

Traditionally, AI models required vast amounts of labelled data to perform tasks effectively. However, modern text generation models exhibit few-shot and zero-shot learning capabilities, meaning they can generate text with minimal or even no prior examples. This allows businesses and individuals to deploy AI for various writing tasks without extensive training datasets.

c) Improved Context Retention

Early AI models struggled with maintaining context over long passages of text. However, recent advancements in memory and attention mechanisms have significantly improved context retention, allowing AI to generate long-form content that remains coherent and logically structured.

d) Style Adaptability

Modern text generation systems can adapt to different writing styles, tones, and formats. Whether it's generating a formal business report, a creative short story, or a conversational customer service response, AI can tailor text to meet specific requirements.

3. Industry Applications of AI-Generated Text

The impact of AI-powered text generation spans multiple industries, enhancing efficiency, creativity, and engagement.

a) Journalism and Content Creation

Media houses and content creators have leveraged AI to generate news articles, blog posts, and reports. Automated journalism allows news organisations to quickly produce fact-based reports on topics such as financial markets and

sports events. AI-generated content also helps bloggers
and marketers scale their content strategies efficiently.

b) Marketing and Advertising

Brands use AI to craft compelling marketing copy, social
media posts, and email campaigns. AI-driven copywriting
tools enable businesses to generate persuasive, high-
converting content, personalised for different target
audiences.

c) Customer Support and Chatbots

Conversational AI has revolutionised customer service by
providing instant, accurate, and human-like responses. AI
chatbots enhance user experience by handling routine
queries, troubleshooting issues, and even offering
personalised recommendations.

d) Education and E-Learning

AI-generated text aids in creating educational materials,
summarising complex concepts, and providing
personalised tutoring. Students benefit from AI-driven
content that simplifies learning and adapts to their
individual needs.

e) Legal and Technical Documentation

AI is increasingly being used to draft legal contracts, policy
documents, and technical manuals. This reduces the
workload for professionals while ensuring accuracy and
compliance with industry standards.

CHAPTER 8: ETHICAL, LEGAL AND SECURITY CONCERNS

Learning Objective

This chapter addresses ethical, legal, and security challenges in generative AI, including bias, fairness, misinformation, intellectual property, privacy, and industry impact. It highlights AI regulation, self-governance, environmental concerns, and responsible AI practices to ensure fairness, transparency, and accountability in AI-generated content.

8.1 Bias and Fairness in AI-Generated Data

AI systems become more integrated into everyday life, concerns regarding bias and fairness have emerged. These issues can have significant ethical, social, and legal implications. Understanding bias in AI-generated data and ensuring fairness in algorithmic decisions are critical steps in fostering responsible AI development.

1. Understanding Bias in AI

Bias in AI refers to systematic errors in data processing that result in unfair outcomes, often disproportionately affecting certain groups. These biases can emerge from multiple sources:

   a. **Data Bias**: AI systems learn from historical data, which may reflect existing societal prejudices. If the

188

training data contains biased representations, the
AI model will inherit and perpetuate these biases.

b. **Algorithmic Bias**: Some AI models prioritise
certain types of data over others, leading to skewed
predictions. This can occur due to flaws in
algorithm design or inappropriate weighting of
variables.

c. **Human Bias**: Since AI models are created and
trained by humans, unconscious biases may
influence the selection of training data and the way
algorithms are structured.

d. **Selection Bias**: When data used for training is not
representative of the entire population, the AI
model may make inaccurate or unfair predictions
for underrepresented groups.

e. **Automation Bias**: This occurs when people place
excessive trust in AI-generated decisions, assuming
they are inherently objective, even when they are
flawed.

2. **Fairness in AI**

Ensuring fairness in AI requires proactive measures to
mitigate bias and create more equitable outcomes. Fairness
can be categorised into different dimensions:

a. **Demographic Fairness**: Ensuring that AI systems
do not disproportionately disadvantage specific
demographic groups.

    b. **Procedural Fairness**: Transparency in AI decision-making processes, ensuring accountability and explainability.

    c. **Outcome Fairness**: Ensuring that AI-generated outcomes are equitable across different groups and do not reinforce existing inequalities.

    d. **Contextual Fairness**: Considering the specific use case of AI applications to determine what fairness means in a given scenario.

3. **Strategies for Mitigating Bias in AI**

To create fair AI systems, developers, researchers, and organisations must adopt strategies that address bias at multiple levels:

a) **Diverse and Representative Data**

Using diverse datasets that accurately reflect different demographic groups helps reduce data bias. Regular audits and updates to datasets can prevent outdated or skewed information from influencing AI models.

b) **Bias Detection and Evaluation**

Techniques such as fairness metrics, adversarial testing, and counterfactual analysis can help identify and measure bias in AI models. These tools enable developers to assess whether an algorithm systematically favours or disadvantages any group.

c) **Algorithmic Transparency and Explainability**

Ensuring that AI decision-making processes are interpretable allows stakeholders to understand how decisions are made. Techniques such as explainable AI (XAI) help in making AI systems more transparent and accountable.

d) Fairness Constraints in Model Development

AI models can be designed with fairness constraints that ensure equitable treatment across different groups. For example, fairness-aware machine learning techniques adjust model outputs to prevent disparate impacts.

e) Regulatory and Ethical Compliance

Governments and organisations should implement policies and ethical guidelines to regulate AI development. Frameworks such as the European Union's AI Act and ethical AI principles from organisations like the IEEE provide guidance on responsible AI usage.

f) Human Oversight and Continuous Monitoring

AI should not operate in isolation; human oversight is essential to detect and correct biases. Continuous monitoring of AI systems in real-world applications helps to identify unintended consequences and make necessary adjustments.

8.2   Responsible AI

An emerging field of AI governance is responsible AI. The term "responsible" is used to refer to both ethics and the democratisation of AI.

Bias is often introduced by the data sets used to train machine learning (ML) models used in artificial intelligence. There are two primary methods by which bias is introduced into these models: incomplete or defective data, or the biases of those who train the ML model. Biased AI programs have the potential to harm or adversely impact people. For instance, it may unjustly deny credit applications or, in the medical field, misdiagnose a patient.

1. Principles of Responsible AI

A set of guidelines that may vary from company to company should be adhered to by AI and machine learning models.

For instance, both Google and Microsoft adhere to their own set of values. Furthermore, a 1.0 version of the Artificial Intelligence Risk Management Framework issued by the National Institute of Standards and Technology (NIST) adheres to many of the same guidelines as those listed by Google and Microsoft. Among NIST's seven guiding principles are the following:

a. **Valid and reliable:** In various and unforeseen situations, responsible AI systems need to be able to continue operating without experiencing any problems.

b. **Safe:** Responsible AI must protect the environment, property, and human life.

c. **Secure and resilient:** Appropriate AI systems need to be safe and strong against possible dangers, such hostile assaults. AI systems that are responsible must be designed to prevent, defend against, and react to assaults while also having the capacity to bounce back from them.

d. **Accountable and transparent:** The goal of more transparency is to increase confidence in the AI system while also making it simpler to address issues related to the output of AI models. Developers are required under this concept to assume accountability for their AI systems.

e. **Explainable and interpretable:** Explainability and interpretability are designed to provide detailed information about how well an AI system works and how reliable it is. For instance, explainable AI explains to people how and why the system produced its results.

f. **Privacy-enhanced:** Practices that protect end users' autonomy, identity, and dignity are enforced under the privacy principle. Values like control, anonymity, and secrecy must guide the development and implementation of responsible AI systems.

g. **Fair with harmful bias managed:** Eliminating AI prejudice and discrimination is the main goal of fairness. It makes an effort to guarantee justice and equality, which is a challenging undertaking since these ideals vary throughout organisations and their cultures.

2. Designing Responsible AI

AI models have to be developed with specific objectives that centre on developing a model in a manner that is secure, reliable, and moral. To make sure a company is dedicated to offering objective, reliable AI technology, constant examination is essential. An organisation must adhere to a maturity model while developing and deploying an AI system in order to accomplish this.

Fundamentally, development standards that emphasise responsible design principles are the foundation of responsible AI. The following requirements have to be included into these corporate-wide AI development guidelines:

a. Shared code repositories.
b. Approved model architectures.
c. Sanctioned variables.
d. Established bias testing methodologies to help determine the validity of tests for AI systems.
e. Stability standards for active machine learning models to ensure AI programming works as intended.

3. Challenges in Implementing Responsible AI

The process of implementing responsible AI rules and frameworks is often slowed down by important issues and concerns. Among these challenges are the following:

a. **Security and privacy:** Companies that gather information for AI model training may need private information about specific people. Although it may be challenging to distinguish private information from public information, responsible AI principles seek to address data privacy, security, and protection.

b. **Data bias:** To prevent biases, training data should be carefully obtained and examined, although biases are sometimes difficult to identify. There is no one-size-fits-all method; it takes time and effort to remove biases from inputs and data sets.

c. **Compliance:** Businesses must keep an eye out for new restrictions and make sure their AI policies are simple to update as laws and regulations continue to change at the local, state, federal, and international levels.

d. **Training:** Business owners need to be aware of who is in charge of managing AI systems and make sure they are properly educated. Legal, marketing, human resources, and other departments and stakeholders may need training in addition to technical teams.

8.3   Intellectual Property and the Generative AI Platform

In simple terms, intellectual property (IP) encompasses the intangible creations of humans, including "ideas, inventions, creative works, logos, brand names, and more". Intellectual property rights (IPR), which are designed to safeguard creators and stop unauthorised use of their works, are a similar idea.

There are currently a number of ongoing legal actions against companies that have provided AI picture generation, AI text generation, and AI code generation tools, and more will surely come as a result of the fast emergence of generative AI and its associated complicated intellectual property issues.

Though this is just the beginning, the use of IPR-protected information in model training has been the primary focus of these litigation up to this point. Numerous more IP hazards are associated with generative AI:

1. Training Data Risks

Using IP-protected data to train AI models is one of the most often recognised concerns. Although this concern is not exclusive to generative AI, it has grown in importance as artists see their creations being copied in generative AI model outputs and feel that their employment are in jeopardy.

Businesses that create generative AI models are coming under fire for training their models on copyrighted content without the owners' consent, and it's not clear whether current exclusions like fair use would apply in these situations. There is now a range of methods, from rigorous limitations and fully transparent disclosure of training material to almost unlimited use of copyrighted works, and several nations and international groups are actively working on relevant recommendations and regulations.

2. Model Output Risks

Adding to the risks associated with training data, generative AI models may generate outputs that, often without alerting model users, integrate or otherwise differ from protected works. Then, if these outputs are employed in commercial activities, these users—who may be anybody from freelancers to firm employees—face possible consequences. The exact level of "derivedness" required for a model output to pose a danger to the user is still unknown and will probably only be made explicit by legal action or legislation. The intellectual property rights (IPRs) that may be applied to generative AI outputs remain unclear as well, given that they are not fully human-made.

3. Software Licencing Risks

Software licencing risks are similar to model output hazards that occur when developers employ AI to produce usable code. It could be necessary for new software to appropriately represent the license or licenses linked to the code in the training data if a generative AI model that was trained on code with attached licenses is later used to create comparable code that is integrated into new software. For instance, under severe circumstances, copyleft licenses can mandate that commercial software be declared open source as well.

4.   Data Leakage and Trade Secret Risks

Depending on the product and model, generative AI models may be continuously trained using input data; however, once learnt, there is a chance that the data may be replicated for other users. This makes it difficult to protect sensitive and private information when using generative AI models and products. In fact, there have been cases where companies have banned ChatGPT after employees used private company information in generative AI prompts and it was later discovered that the information had leaked outside the company.

5.   Inventorship Risks

AI has already been utilised to assist in the development of new innovations in several domains, such as medication design. It is still uncertain how—or even if—AI may be portrayed as having contributed to a claimed idea since the majority of IP offices need a human inventor to be mentioned on a patent. This may sound harmless, but if a court reviews a patent and determines that it is not primarily the invention of the listed inventor, the patent may be declared invalid.

8.4   Misinformation and Misuse of Generative AI

Alongside generative AI benefits, generative AI presents significant risks, particularly in the spread of misinformation and its potential for misuse. As AI-generated content becomes increasingly indistinguishable from human-created material, concerns over ethical implications, security threats, and societal impact grow ever more pressing.

1. The Rise of Misinformation through Generative AI

One of the primary concerns regarding generative AI is its role in the proliferation of misinformation. AI models can generate highly convincing fake news articles, manipulated media, and misleading narratives that can easily deceive the public. With the rapid spread of information on social media platforms, such content can gain traction quickly, influencing public opinion and shaping real-world events.

a) Fake News and Disinformation

AI-generated content can be used to create false narratives that appear credible. Malicious actors exploit these capabilities to spread propaganda, influence elections, or manipulate stock markets. Unlike traditional misinformation, AI-driven disinformation can be mass-produced with minimal effort, making it a powerful tool for those with deceptive intentions.

b) Deepfake Technology

Deepfake AI, which generates hyper-realistic synthetic media, has become a major concern. Videos and images manipulated by AI can fabricate events, create false testimonies, or impersonate public figures. This technology poses serious threats in politics, cybersecurity, and even personal privacy, as deepfake videos can be used to blackmail individuals or damage reputations.

c)   Social Media Manipulation

Social media is particularly vulnerable to AI-generated misinformation. Bots and AI-driven accounts can flood platforms with misleading content, amplifying divisive issues and fostering political and social unrest. The ability of generative AI to mimic writing styles and human interactions makes it difficult to distinguish between real users and automated accounts.

2.   The Ethical and Legal Challenges of AI Misuse

With generative AI's potential for misuse, ethical and legal frameworks struggle to keep pace. Issues surrounding accountability, intellectual property, and privacy are among the key challenges facing regulators and technology companies.

a)   Accountability and AI-Generated Content

A critical question in AI ethics is determining responsibility for AI-generated misinformation. Should accountability fall on the developers, the users, or the platforms hosting the content? The absence of clear regulations complicates efforts to hold malicious actors responsible for their actions.

b)   Copyright and Intellectual Property

AI-generated content raises complex intellectual property concerns. Artists, writers, and musicians face challenges when AI creates work that closely resembles human-created pieces. The question of ownership—whether AI-generated works can be copyrighted and who holds the rights—remains unresolved in many jurisdictions.

c) Privacy and Security Risks

Generative AI can be used to create convincing phishing emails, voice synthesis for scams, and impersonation fraud. Such activities threaten cybersecurity and personal privacy, as AI-generated content can deceive individuals into sharing sensitive information or engaging in fraudulent transactions.

8.5   Privacy, Safety, and Security

The rapid advancement of generative artificial intelligence has raised serious concerns about privacy, security, and safety. Addressing these challenges is essential to ensure responsible deployment of AI while protecting individuals, organisations, and society.

1.   Privacy Concerns in Generative AI

Privacy is a fundamental issue in the age of AI. Generative models often rely on vast datasets that include publicly available, proprietary, and sometimes sensitive information. These datasets may inadvertently contain personal data, raising concerns about how information is collected, processed, and utilised.

One of the primary privacy risks involves data leakage. AI models, particularly large language models (LLMs), have been shown to memorise and reproduce training data, sometimes exposing sensitive personal details. If a model is trained on confidential medical records, financial information, or private conversations, it may generate outputs that reveal such data when queried in specific ways.

Furthermore, user interactions with AI systems can themselves be a source of privacy risks. Chatbots and other generative AI applications often collect input data to improve performance. However, without robust data protection measures, this information could be exploited for surveillance, targeted advertising, or even malicious activities. Users may not always be aware of what data is being stored, how it is being used, or whether they have control over its deletion.

Addressing these concerns requires stringent data protection policies, clear user consent mechanisms, and compliance with regulations such as the General Data Protection Regulation (GDPR) and India's Digital Personal Data Protection Act (DPDPA). Organisations must adopt privacy-preserving techniques, including differential privacy, data anonymisation, and federated learning, to mitigate risks while maintaining AI's capabilities.

2. Safety Issues with Generative AI

Ensuring the safety of generative AI is paramount, as these models can be misused in various ways, leading to ethical, social, and economic harm. One pressing issue is the generation of misleading or harmful content. AI-generated deepfakes, for example, can be used to manipulate public opinion, spread misinformation, or defame individuals. Malicious actors have leveraged AI to create convincing fake news, impersonate real individuals, and even automate cyber fraud.

Bias and discrimination are also major safety concerns. AI models learn from historical data, which may reflect societal prejudices. If not carefully managed, these biases can manifest in AI-generated content, reinforcing stereotypes and unfair treatment in areas such as recruitment, lending, and law enforcement.

Another critical aspect of AI safety involves hallucinations—instances where generative AI produces incorrect or nonsensical information. Unlike traditional software, AI models do not "know" facts but instead generate probabilistic outputs based on patterns in training data. This can lead to AI confidently presenting falsehoods, posing risks in fields such as healthcare, law, and scientific research.

To mitigate these risks, AI developers must implement rigorous testing, ethical AI principles, and transparency in model development. Responsible AI frameworks should include content moderation, real-time monitoring, and user feedback mechanisms to prevent the spread of harmful or misleading content.

3. Security Risks in Generative AI

Security threats in generative AI extend beyond data privacy and safety, encompassing vulnerabilities that can be exploited by cybercriminals and adversaries. One of the primary concerns is adversarial attacks, where attackers manipulate input data to deceive AI models into generating undesirable or harmful outputs. These attacks can be used to bypass content filters, alter AI-generated recommendations, or exploit security flaws in automated decision-making systems.

Phishing attacks and automated fraud also benefit from AI-generated content. Cybercriminals can use AI to create highly convincing emails, voice recordings, and text messages, making phishing scams harder to detect. With the rise of AI-generated impersonation, businesses and individuals face greater risks of fraud, identity theft, and financial crimes.

Additionally, the increasing integration of generative AI in critical infrastructure, such as banking, healthcare, and cybersecurity, raises concerns about its robustness against hacking attempts. If malicious actors gain access to AI-powered systems, they could manipulate financial transactions, tamper with medical diagnoses, or disrupt essential services.

To enhance AI security, organisations must prioritise robust cybersecurity measures, including encrypted data storage, secure API access, and regular security audits. AI developers should also implement adversarial training—

techniques that expose AI models to potential attacks during development to improve their resilience against real-world threats.

8.6 Generative AI's Impact on Jobs and Industry

AI presents numerous opportunities for businesses and professionals; it also raises concerns about job displacement and evolving skill requirements. Understanding the implications of generative AI on jobs and industries is crucial for individuals and organisations striving to adapt to this technological revolution.

1. Generative AI is Transforming Industries

Generative AI has already made significant inroads into various industries, enhancing efficiency, reducing costs, and enabling innovation. Some of the most affected sectors include:

a) Media and Content Creation

The rise of AI-driven tools, such as ChatGPT, DALL-E, and Midjourney, has revolutionised the way content is generated. Writers, graphic designers, and video editors now have AI-powered assistants that help streamline their creative processes. Automated content creation allows businesses to scale their marketing efforts rapidly, producing blogs, advertisements, and social media posts in a fraction of the time.

However, this advancement also challenges traditional creative roles. While AI can generate text, images, and videos at an impressive speed, human oversight remains essential to ensure originality, quality, and ethical considerations. Rather than replacing creative professionals, AI is shifting their roles towards more strategic and editorial functions.

b) Software Development and IT

Generative AI is revolutionising the IT sector, particularly in coding and software development. AI-powered tools can generate code, debug software, and assist in project management, significantly reducing development time. Platforms like GitHub Copilot and OpenAI Codex enable programmers to automate repetitive coding tasks and focus on complex problem-solving.

Despite these advancements, AI is unlikely to replace software engineers entirely. Instead, it is becoming an essential assistant that enhances productivity. Developers who embrace AI tools will have a competitive edge, as they can delegate routine coding to AI while focusing on innovation and system architecture.

c) Customer Service and Chatbots

Customer service has seen a dramatic shift with the adoption of AI-powered chatbots and virtual assistants. These tools provide instant responses to customer queries, reducing wait times and improving user experience.

Companies leverage AI to handle routine inquiries, freeing up human agents to tackle complex or sensitive issues.

While AI-driven automation reduces the demand for entry-level customer service roles, it also creates new opportunities in AI training, bot management, and customer experience design. Professionals in this field will need to acquire skills in AI integration and human-AI collaboration.

d) Healthcare and Pharmaceuticals

The healthcare industry is benefiting from generative AI in diagnostics, drug discovery, and patient care. AI models can analyse medical images, predict diseases, and even assist in developing new drugs. Pharmaceutical companies use AI to accelerate research, reducing the time required to bring new treatments to market.

Despite these innovations, human expertise remains indispensable. Doctors, researchers, and healthcare professionals work alongside AI, leveraging its insights while making critical decisions based on ethical, emotional, and contextual factors that AI lacks.

e) Manufacturing and Automation

Manufacturing has long been at the forefront of automation, and generative AI is further optimising production lines, supply chain management, and quality control. AI-powered robotics are handling complex assembly tasks, predictive maintenance is minimising downtime, and AI-generated designs are improving product efficiency.

While some manual jobs may decline, AI is also creating demand for engineers, robotics specialists, and AI system integrators. Workers skilled in AI-driven technologies will find new opportunities in maintaining and programming automated systems.

2. The Impact on Jobs

The integration of generative AI into industries inevitably affects the job market in both positive and challenging ways. Various impacts include:

a) Job Displacement vs. Job Creation

One of the most debated aspects of AI adoption is its potential to replace human jobs. While some routine and repetitive tasks are being automated, AI is also creating new roles that require human intervention. Jobs in AI ethics, prompt engineering, AI model training, and system monitoring are emerging as businesses seek to optimise AI usage responsibly.

b) Shift in Skill Requirements

The increasing reliance on AI necessitates a shift in skill sets. Traditional job roles are evolving, requiring professionals to acquire new competencies. Critical thinking, problem-solving, AI literacy, and data analysis are becoming essential skills in the modern workforce. Employees who upskill and adapt to these changes will remain valuable in their respective fields.

c)   Rise of Hybrid Roles

Rather than replacing human workers entirely, AI is fostering hybrid roles where professionals collaborate with AI tools. For example, journalists use AI-generated drafts to enhance their writing, financial analysts use AI to detect trends, and educators use AI to personalise learning experiences. These hybrid roles require individuals to understand AI's capabilities and limitations while applying human expertise to enhance outcomes.

d)   Entrepreneurial Opportunities

Generative AI is lowering the barriers to entry for entrepreneurship. Small businesses and independent professionals can leverage AI for marketing, content creation, customer support, and automation, enabling them to compete with larger enterprises. Startups are also emerging in AI-driven industries, offering innovative solutions across various sectors.

8.7   The Dependency on AI

The increasing reliance on AI is evident in sectors such as healthcare, finance, education, and entertainment, among others. While AI offers numerous benefits, excessive dependence on it presents both opportunities and risks.

1.   The Benefits of AI Dependency

The advantages of AI are undeniable, leading to greater efficiency, accuracy, and accessibility across various domains. Businesses and individuals alike rely on AI-driven technologies to simplify tasks, analyse vast amounts of data, and make informed decisions. The following are some key benefits:

a)   Increased Efficiency and Productivity

AI-driven automation has revolutionised industries by handling repetitive and time-consuming tasks with remarkable speed and accuracy. In manufacturing, AI-powered robots assemble products efficiently, reducing production costs and human error. Similarly, AI algorithms streamline business operations, optimising supply chains, customer service, and logistics.

b)   Improved Decision-Making

AI's ability to process and analyse large datasets enables organisations to make data-driven decisions with precision. In financial markets, AI-powered trading algorithms assess risks and execute transactions within milliseconds, leading to more informed investment strategies. In healthcare, AI assists in diagnosing diseases, predicting patient outcomes, and recommending personalised treatment plans.

c)   Enhanced Personalisation

AI has significantly improved user experiences by providing personalised recommendations in e-commerce, entertainment, and social media. Streaming platforms use AI to suggest content based on viewing history, while online retailers recommend products tailored to individual preferences. This level of customisation enhances customer satisfaction and engagement.

d) Better Accessibility and Inclusion

AI-driven technologies have improved accessibility for individuals with disabilities. Voice recognition software, speech-to-text applications, and AI-powered assistants enable greater independence for those with visual or motor impairments. AI also facilitates language translation, bridging communication gaps between people from different linguistic backgrounds.

2. The Risks of AI Dependency

While AI offers numerous benefits, an overreliance on it can pose significant risks. Dependency on AI without adequate human oversight may lead to ethical dilemmas, job displacement, security concerns, and a reduction in human cognitive abilities.

a) Job Displacement and Economic Impact

Automation powered by AI has led to job losses in various industries, particularly in manufacturing, customer service, and transportation. As machines replace human workers in repetitive and routine tasks, concerns about unemployment and economic disparities have risen. While AI creates new job opportunities in tech-driven sectors, there is a growing need for workforce reskilling and adaptation to evolving job roles.

b) Ethical and Bias Concerns

AI algorithms are trained on historical data, which may contain inherent biases. If not carefully monitored, AI systems can reinforce and perpetuate discrimination in hiring practices, law enforcement, and financial services. Algorithmic bias has been a growing concern, as it can lead to unfair treatment of certain groups based on race, gender, or socio-economic status.

c) Loss of Human Skills and Critical Thinking

Excessive reliance on AI for decision-making may lead to a decline in human cognitive abilities. When individuals depend on AI for problem-solving and information retrieval, their capacity for critical thinking and analytical reasoning may diminish. This trend is particularly concerning in education, where students rely on AI-powered tools rather than developing independent problem-solving skills.

d) Security and Privacy Risks

AI-driven technologies are vulnerable to cyber threats and data breaches. Hackers can exploit AI systems to manipulate information, spread misinformation, or gain unauthorised access to sensitive data. The increasing use of AI in surveillance raises concerns about privacy, as governments and corporations collect vast amounts of personal data, potentially leading to misuse or unethical surveillance practices.

8.8   Environmental Concerns

Generative AI capabilities have also raised significant environmental concerns. With the increasing reliance on AI models, especially at scale, comes substantial energy consumption, carbon emissions, and electronic waste. These environmental issues require urgent attention to ensure that technological progress does not come at the cost of ecological sustainability.

1.   Energy Consumption and Carbon Footprint

One of the most pressing environmental concerns associated with generative AI is its high energy consumption. Training and running large AI models, such as OpenAI's GPT series or Google's DeepMind projects, require vast amounts of computational power. These models are trained using high-performance data centres that consume substantial electricity, often relying on fossil fuel-based energy sources.

A single training run of a sophisticated AI model can use as much energy as hundreds of homes consume in a year. Studies have estimated that training a large neural network can generate carbon emissions equivalent to multiple long-haul flights. As AI adoption grows, so does its environmental impact, exacerbating global climate challenges.

2.   Data Centres and Water Usage

AI-driven data centres require extensive cooling mechanisms to maintain optimal performance. This cooling process involves significant water usage, adding another layer of environmental concern. Many AI data centres are located in regions already facing water scarcity, intensifying existing resource challenges. As demand for AI services increases, so does the pressure on water supplies, raising ethical questions about the trade-offs between technological progress and natural resource conservation.

3. Electronic Waste and Hardware Requirements

The hardware requirements for AI processing are another environmental challenge. The production of high-performance GPUs (Graphics Processing Units) and TPUs (Tensor Processing Units) needed for AI training involves mining and processing rare earth metals. This process has its own environmental toll, including habitat destruction, soil and water pollution, and carbon emissions from mining operations.

Moreover, the rapid advancement of AI technology results in frequent hardware upgrades, contributing to electronic waste. The disposal of outdated or inefficient computing equipment further strains waste management systems, as many of these electronic components contain hazardous materials that can contaminate ecosystems if not properly recycled.

4. Sustainability Measures and Potential Solutions

To mitigate the environmental impact of generative AI, companies and researchers must explore sustainable solutions. Several measures can be adopted to reduce AI's carbon footprint and promote responsible technological development.

a. **Energy-Efficient AI Models** – Researchers are developing AI models that require less computational power without compromising performance. Techniques such as model pruning, knowledge distillation, and optimised algorithms help reduce energy consumption while maintaining efficiency.

b. **Renewable Energy Adoption** – Transitioning AI data centres to renewable energy sources, such as solar and wind power, can significantly cut carbon emissions. Companies like Google and Microsoft have already committed to powering their AI operations with clean energy.

c. **Improved Cooling Systems** – Innovations in cooling technologies, such as liquid cooling and advanced air circulation systems, can reduce the water and energy demands of data centres.

d. **Sustainable Hardware Practices** – Developing AI processors with longer lifespans and improved efficiency can help minimise electronic waste. Additionally, promoting responsible recycling practices and adopting a circular economy approach for AI hardware can alleviate environmental concerns.

e. **Regulatory and Industry Collaboration** – Governments and industry leaders must work together to establish environmental regulations for AI development. Policies promoting sustainability, carbon neutrality, and ethical AI usage can ensure a balanced approach to technological progress and ecological responsibility.

8.9   AI Oversight and Self-Regulation

Artificial Intelligence (AI) has emerged as a transformative force across industries, revolutionising everything from healthcare and finance to marketing and governance. However, as AI systems become more powerful and deeply integrated into daily life, concerns regarding their ethical implications, potential biases, and unintended consequences have grown.

1.   The Need for AI Oversight

AI oversight refers to the frameworks, policies, and mechanisms put in place to monitor and guide AI development and usage. Given AI's potential for both positive and harmful outcomes, oversight ensures that AI systems remain fair, accountable, and transparent. Several factors contribute to the need for robust oversight:

a.   **Ethical Considerations** – AI-driven decisions can have profound ethical implications, particularly in sensitive areas such as healthcare, hiring, and law enforcement. Without proper oversight, biases in AI models can perpetuate discrimination and reinforce systemic inequalities.

b. **Security and Privacy Risks** – AI systems process
vast amounts of data, often including personal and
sensitive information. Ensuring that AI adheres to
strict data protection regulations is essential to
prevent breaches and misuse.

c. **Accountability and Transparency** – Many AI
systems function as 'black boxes,' making it
difficult to understand how they arrive at their
conclusions. Transparency in AI decision-making is
critical for ensuring accountability and public trust.

d. **Mitigating Misinformation** – AI-driven content
generation and recommendation algorithms
influence public opinion and information
dissemination. Without oversight, there is a risk of
spreading misinformation and propaganda at an
unprecedented scale.

2. **Approaches to AI Oversight**

AI oversight is achieved through a combination of
regulatory frameworks, industry best practices, and ethical
guidelines. Different countries and organisations adopt
varied approaches to AI governance, with some
prioritising strict regulatory control and others advocating
for self-regulation.

a) **Government Regulations**

Governments worldwide are developing laws and policies
to govern AI. The European Union's AI Act, for instance,
classifies AI applications based on risk levels and imposes
stricter requirements on high-risk AI systems. Similarly,

countries such as the United States, China, and the United Kingdom are exploring regulatory measures to ensure AI aligns with public interest.

b) Industry Standards and Guidelines

Tech companies and industry bodies play a crucial role in AI oversight by establishing voluntary guidelines and ethical frameworks. Organisations such as the Institute of Electrical and Electronics Engineers (IEEE) and the Partnership on AI promote responsible AI development by setting standards on fairness, accountability, and bias mitigation.

c) Independent AI Audits

Third-party audits assess AI systems to ensure they comply with ethical and legal standards. Independent oversight bodies evaluate AI models for bias, transparency, and security risks, providing recommendations to improve accountability.

d) Public and Stakeholder Involvement

Public participation in AI governance ensures that AI technologies align with societal values and do not solely serve corporate interests. Citizen panels, advisory boards, and collaborative policymaking efforts can help shape AI regulations that benefit everyone.

3. The Role of Self-Regulation in AI Governance

Self-regulation involves AI developers and organisations voluntarily adopting ethical guidelines, best practices, and

accountability measures without direct government
intervention. While self-regulation cannot entirely replace
formal oversight, it serves as a proactive approach to
responsible AI development.

a. **Ethical AI Frameworks** – Companies are
increasingly incorporating ethical AI principles into
their workflows. Google's AI Principles,
Microsoft's Responsible AI framework, and
OpenAI's policies on AI safety exemplify self-
regulatory efforts within the industry.

b. **Bias and Fairness Assessments** – AI developers
conduct fairness assessments to identify and
mitigate biases in machine learning models,
ensuring equitable treatment across different
demographics.

c. **Transparency Initiatives** – Open-source AI
research, model documentation, and explainable AI
techniques improve transparency and foster trust
in AI systems.

d. **Collaboration and Knowledge Sharing** – Industry
players collaborate to share best practices and
findings, promoting a culture of responsible AI
innovation.

8.10 Regulatory Challenges

The rapid adoption of generative AI has also raised
significant regulatory concerns globally, and India is no
exception. While the Indian government acknowledges the

potential of AI, the regulatory landscape remains unclear, presenting several challenges.

1. Absence of a Comprehensive Legal Framework

One of the primary challenges in regulating generative AI in India is the absence of a dedicated legal framework. Unlike the European Union, which has introduced the AI Act, India has yet to formulate a structured approach to AI governance. The current regulatory environment consists of a patchwork of existing laws, such as the Information Technology Act, 2000, and the upcoming Digital India Act, which do not specifically address generative AI's unique challenges. This lack of clear guidelines creates uncertainty for businesses, developers, and users.

2. Data Privacy and Security Concerns

Generative AI models require vast amounts of data for training, which raises concerns about data privacy and security. The Digital Personal Data Protection Act, 2023, provides a legal framework for data governance, but its applicability to AI-generated content remains unclear. Questions arise regarding how AI firms should handle user-generated data, whether AI-generated content should be considered personal data, and how to ensure data protection while maintaining innovation. Moreover, there is the risk of AI models unintentionally memorising sensitive information, leading to potential data breaches.

3. Misinformation and Deepfake Regulation

Generative AI has enabled the creation of highly realistic
deepfakes and synthetic media, posing risks of
misinformation, fraud, and reputational damage. The
spread of AI-generated fake news can influence elections,
manipulate public opinion, and cause societal harm. While
the Information Technology (Intermediary Guidelines and
Digital Media Ethics Code) Rules, 2021, address
misinformation to some extent, there is no specific
mechanism for handling AI-generated deepfakes.
Regulating such content without infringing on free speech
is a complex challenge that Indian lawmakers must
address.

4. Intellectual Property and Copyright Issues

Generative AI raises serious concerns regarding
intellectual property (IP) rights. Content generated by AI
often resembles existing copyrighted works, leading to
potential copyright infringements. The Indian Copyright
Act, 1957, does not currently address AI-generated works,
creating legal ambiguity regarding ownership and
liability. Should AI-generated works be considered
original creations? If so, who owns them—the developer,
the user, or the AI itself? These unresolved questions make
it difficult for businesses to commercialise AI-generated
content without legal risks.

5. Ethical and Bias Concerns

AI models, including generative AI, can perpetuate biases
present in their training data. This has ethical implications,
particularly in a diverse country like India, where socio-

economic, linguistic, and cultural factors must be considered. If AI-generated content reinforces stereotypes or discriminates against certain groups, it can lead to reputational damage and legal challenges. There is a need for regulatory oversight to ensure AI systems are fair, unbiased, and transparent in their decision-making processes.

6. Compliance Burden for Businesses and Startups

India has a growing AI startup ecosystem, but regulatory uncertainty poses a significant compliance burden. Small and medium-sized enterprises (SMEs) may struggle to navigate evolving legal requirements, especially if strict AI regulations are implemented without clear guidelines. Overregulation could stifle innovation, while under-regulation could lead to legal risks and unethical AI deployment. Striking a balance is crucial to fostering AI-driven entrepreneurship while ensuring responsible AI use.

7. Accountability and Liability Issues

Determining accountability in cases where generative AI causes harm is another significant challenge. If an AI model generates defamatory or harmful content, who is held responsible—the developer, the platform hosting the AI, or the end user? Without clear liability provisions, legal disputes could arise, leading to uncertainty for businesses and consumers. Establishing a regulatory framework that delineates responsibility in AI-related disputes is crucial for legal clarity.

CHAPTER 9: FUTURE OF GENERATIVE AI

Learning Objective

This chapter explores the future trajectory of generative AI, including the path toward Artificial General Intelligence (AGI), autonomous AI agents, humanoid robots, and broader AI integration. It examines the limitless potential of AI advancements, the role of human optimism, and AI's transformative impact on industries and society.

9.1   Artificial General Intelligence in Sight

The domain of Artificial General Intelligence (AGI) encompasses theoretical research in AI, aiming to develop software that possesses human-like intelligence and the capacity for self-directed learning. The objective is for the software to execute tasks for which it has not been specifically trained or developed.

Existing artificial intelligence technologies operate within a defined range of parameters. For instance, AI models that have been taught to recognise and create images are unable to create webpages. The pursuit of AGI is theoretical, aiming to create AI systems that have autonomous self-control, a certain level of self-understanding, and the capability to acquire new skills.

Complex problems can be solved in settings and contexts that were not included during its creation. The idea of AGI possessing human-like abilities continues to be a theoretical notion and an objective of research.

1. Types of Artificial General Intelligence (AGI) Research

Researchers in computer science and artificial intelligence are persistently advancing theoretical frameworks while addressing the unresolved challenge of AGI. Several high-level approaches have been defined that have emerged in the field of AGI research and are categorised as follows:

a. **Symbolic**: A symbolic approach to AGI posits that symbolic thought is fundamental to human general intelligence and is what enables the broadest generalisation capabilities.

b. **Emergentist**: An emergentist perspective on AGI emphasises that the human brain consists of basic components (neurones) that intricately self-organise in response to bodily experiences. It may be inferred that a comparable form of intelligence could arise from the reconstruction of a similar framework.

c. **Hybrid**: The term hybrid approach to AGI implies that the brain functions as a hybrid system, where various components and principles collaborate to produce an outcome that surpasses the mere aggregation of its individual elements. The nature of hybrid AGI research encompasses a broad range of approaches.

d. **Universalist**: A Universalist approach to AGI focusses on the mathematical core of general intelligence, suggesting that once AGI is addressed in theory, the principles derived from that solution can be adapted and applied to its actual development.

2. **Challenges in Artificial General Intelligence Research**

Computer scientists encounter various challenges in the development of AGI.

a) Make connections

Present AI models are confined to their particular areas and are unable to establish links across different domains. Nevertheless, individuals are capable of transferring knowledge and experience from one area to a different one. For instance, game designers use educational ideas to create captivating learning environments. Individuals are capable of applying the knowledge gained from theoretical education to practical situations in life. Nevertheless, deep learning models necessitate extensive training using particular datasets to function dependably with unknown data.

b) Emotional intelligence

Deep learning models suggest the potential for AGI, yet they have not yet shown the genuine creativity inherent to humans. Emotional thinking is essential for creativity, a quality that current neural network architectures have not yet been able to replicate. Humans engage in conversations influenced by their emotional perceptions, whereas NLP models produce text outputs derived from the linguistic datasets and patterns on which they have been trained.

c) Sensory perception

AGI necessitates that AI systems engage physically with the outside environment. In addition to its robotic capabilities, the system needs to understand the world in a manner similar to humans. Current computer technologies require additional development to accurately distinguish shapes, colours, tastes, smells, and sounds in a manner similar to humans.

9.2   What Is Next in Generative AI?

As advancements in artificial intelligence continue, the future of generative AI is poised to redefine how individuals and businesses interact with technology. The next phase of development will focus on improving efficiency, creativity, and ethical considerations. Here's what to expect in the coming years.

1.   More Sophisticated and Context-Aware Models

Current generative AI models, such as GPT-4 and DALL·E, have demonstrated impressive capabilities, but they still struggle with context retention and nuanced reasoning. Future AI models will likely be designed to exhibit better comprehension, logical consistency, and reduced hallucinations. Researchers are working on techniques such as retrieval-augmented generation (RAG) and fine-tuned contextual embeddings to make AI responses more accurate and context-aware. These enhancements will enable AI to engage in more meaningful, human-like interactions.

2. Multimodal AI Systems

The future of generative AI lies in the seamless integration of multiple data modalities. Instead of handling text, images, audio, and video separately, next-generation AI will process and generate content across various formats simultaneously. Companies like OpenAI and Google DeepMind are already exploring models that can combine text with visual elements, creating richer and more interactive digital experiences. This evolution will enable applications such as advanced video editing, realistic virtual assistants, and enhanced augmented reality experiences.

3. AI-Generated Content with Improved Authenticity

While generative AI has been instrumental in content creation, it has also raised concerns about misinformation and deepfakes. To address this, future developments will focus on improving watermarking techniques, authenticity verification, and ethical AI practices. Researchers are developing AI models that can detect synthetic content and provide transparency about AI-generated materials. These advancements will be crucial in maintaining trust in AI-generated content.

4. Customisable and Personalised AI Assistants

AI models are moving beyond general-purpose applications towards more personalised and domain-specific solutions. Future AI will allow users to fine-tune models based on their preferences, industry requirements, or specific use cases. Businesses will benefit from AI tools that understand their unique needs, whether in healthcare, finance, or entertainment. Customisability will enhance user experiences and create AI-driven solutions that feel more intuitive and useful.

5. AI in Software Development and Automation

Generative AI is already assisting in writing and debugging code, but future iterations will take automation to the next level. AI-powered coding assistants will not only generate functional code but also understand software architecture and optimise performance. This will streamline software development, reduce human error, and enable faster deployment of applications. Furthermore, AI will play a significant role in automating repetitive tasks, allowing professionals to focus on more strategic aspects of their work.

6. Ethical AI and Regulatory Developments

As AI becomes more powerful, ethical concerns surrounding bias, privacy, and accountability will take centre stage. Governments and organisations will implement stricter regulations to ensure responsible AI usage. Future AI models will be designed with enhanced fairness, explainability, and compliance mechanisms. AI developers will need to prioritise transparency and ethical considerations to ensure that AI benefits society without causing unintended harm.

7. AI's Role in Scientific Discovery and Research

Beyond creative applications, generative AI is set to revolutionise scientific research. AI-driven models will assist in drug discovery, climate modelling, and material science by generating hypotheses, analysing vast datasets, and proposing innovative solutions. The ability to simulate complex scenarios will accelerate breakthroughs in medicine, engineering, and environmental sustainability.

8. Integration with the Metaverse and Virtual Worlds

As the concept of the metaverse evolves, generative AI will play a key role in shaping virtual environments. AI will generate realistic avatars, immersive landscapes, and interactive narratives, making digital spaces more engaging and dynamic. Businesses and content creators will leverage AI to build expansive, user-generated virtual worlds with minimal effort.

9.3   Scaled Utilisation of AI: Autonomous AI Agents

In the realm of generative AI, autonomous agents refer to systems that utilise the capabilities of Large Language Models (LLMs) to connect various ideas in order to achieve a specific output or objective.

Autonomous AI agents are distinguished from generative AI by their ability to execute multiple tasks sequentially, utilising memory and tools, all without requiring direct human intervention.

The tools utilised by autonomous agents signify the information repositories that are accessed and employed when a prompt is provided. These may encompass the system's LLM or outside resources like websites, databases, or various knowledge bases.

Memory pertains to the accumulated experiences that the autonomous agent possesses, derived from previous prompts and the outputs generated. The autonomous agents are capable of accessing this memory to generate responses that are more contextually relevant for the tasks they need to accomplish.

Through the integration of these tools and memory, LLMs evolve into systems or "agents" capable of operating independently to achieve a specific objective or goal.

1. Autonomous AI Agents vs. Foundation Models

Autonomous agents are created to operate on their own, making choices and performing actions according to their understanding of the surroundings and objectives. The agents can exhibit either reactive or adaptive behaviours, influenced by their complexity.

Conversely, foundation models, such as large language models, undergo pre-training on extensive datasets and

offer general knowledge or abilities that can be tailored for
particular tasks.

Autonomous agents are characterised by their goal-
oriented nature and their emphasis on executing actions,
whereas foundation models are utilised for generating,
classifying, or interpreting data without engaging directly
with their surroundings.

2.   Agentic vs. Non-Agentic AI Chatbots

Autonomous AI chatbots function independently, making
choices and executing tasks without the need for
continuous human supervision. These chatbots have the
ability to adjust to new information, acquire knowledge
from interactions, and carry out complex procedures to
reach defined objectives.

An agentic chatbot could analyse customer enquiries,
provide personalised solutions, and even initiate backend
workflows such as processing refunds or scheduling
appointments, all on its own.

In contrast, non-agentic AI chatbots tend to be more fixed
and focused on specific tasks. Predefined scripts or flows
are utilised to respond to user inputs. Limited adaptability
is provided, along with a lack of decision-making
capabilities beyond the established programmed rules.

Although non-agentic AIs perform well in basic situations
such as responding to frequently asked questions or
assisting users with uncomplicated tasks, they do not

possess the adaptability and problem-solving skills found in agentic chatbots.

9.4   Embodiment of AGI: (Humanoid) Robots

The concept of Artificial General Intelligence (AGI) has long been a subject of fascination, often depicted in science fiction as sentient machines capable of human-like cognition. While AGI remains a theoretical pursuit, significant advancements in artificial intelligence and robotics have brought us closer to its potential realisation. One of the most promising embodiments of AGI is humanoid robots—machines designed to think, learn, and interact in a manner similar to humans.

1.   The Essence of AGI in Humanoid Robots

AGI refers to an artificial intelligence system that can perform any intellectual task a human is capable of, rather than being limited to specific domains like narrow AI. Unlike traditional AI models, which excel in singular tasks such as image recognition or language processing, AGI aims to replicate human-level reasoning, adaptability, and problem-solving abilities.

The embodiment of AGI in humanoid robots serves multiple purposes. Firstly, a humanoid form allows for seamless integration into human environments without the need for significant infrastructure changes. Secondly, it facilitates natural human-robot interactions, enhancing communication and social acceptance. Lastly, by mimicking the human cognitive and motor system, researchers can refine AGI models through real-world interactions rather than solely relying on virtual simulations.

2. Technological Foundations

The development of humanoid robots with AGI capabilities requires the integration of multiple cutting-edge technologies:

a. **Machine Learning and Deep Learning** – Advanced neural networks enable robots to process vast amounts of data, learn from experiences, and make decisions in real time.

b. **Natural Language Processing (NLP)** – Enabling robots to understand and respond to human language naturally is crucial for effective communication.

c. **Computer Vision** – This allows robots to perceive and interpret their surroundings, enabling tasks such as object recognition, facial recognition, and spatial navigation.

d. **Robotics Engineering** – Innovations in materials, actuators, and sensory mechanisms enable humanoid robots to mimic human movements and gestures.

e. **Neuromorphic Computing** – Inspired by the human brain, neuromorphic chips aim to process information more efficiently, bringing robots closer to human-like cognition.

3. Applications and Impact

The integration of AGI into humanoid robots has the potential to transform numerous industries:

a. **Healthcare** – AGI-driven humanoid robots could serve as caregivers, assisting the elderly or disabled with daily tasks and offering companionship.

b. **Customer Service** – Retail, hospitality, and public services could benefit from humanoid robots providing personalised assistance and information.

c. **Manufacturing and Logistics** – Robots with AGI capabilities could adapt to dynamic work environments, optimising production lines and warehouse management.

d. **Education** – As tutors or teaching assistants, humanoid robots could provide interactive and adaptive learning experiences.

e. **Space Exploration** – Autonomous humanoid robots could be deployed for extraterrestrial missions, reducing risks for human astronauts.

9.5 The Human Potential Is Boundless; Optimism Helps

The limitless nature of human potential has long been a subject of fascination. Throughout history, individuals and societies have demonstrated an extraordinary capacity for innovation, creativity, and resilience. With the rapid advancements in technology, particularly in Generative AI, this potential has been further expanded, unlocking new possibilities in ways previously unimaginable. Yet, alongside skill and intelligence, there is another crucial factor that propels human achievement—optimism. A mindset of possibility and progress serves as a catalyst for breakthroughs, allowing individuals to push boundaries and redefine what is possible.

1.   The Expansive Nature of Human Potential

Human potential is not a fixed attribute; rather, it is fluid and ever-evolving. The ability to learn, adapt, and create is at the core of human progress. From scientific discoveries to artistic masterpieces, the spectrum of human capability knows no bounds. Generative AI serves as a perfect example of how human ingenuity continues to stretch the limits of what is conceivable. This technology, inspired by human cognition, can generate art, compose music, and even assist in scientific research, demonstrating that human intelligence, when paired with advanced tools, can achieve remarkable feats.

A defining feature of human potential is its adaptability. The ability to evolve in response to challenges and technological shifts has allowed societies to thrive. The integration of Generative AI into various industries is a testament to this adaptability. From enhancing medical diagnoses to revolutionising content creation, AI has become an extension of human potential, amplifying skills rather than replacing them.

2. The Role of Optimism in Unlocking Potential

While intelligence and skill set the foundation for success, optimism provides the drive needed to pursue ambitious goals. A mindset grounded in positivity fosters resilience, creativity, and an openness to innovation. When individuals believe in the possibility of success, they are more likely to take risks, explore new ideas, and persist through obstacles. This principle applies to the development of Generative AI itself—visionaries in the field saw beyond present limitations and believed in a future where machines could think, learn, and create.

Optimism also plays a crucial role in how people interact with technology. While some fear that AI may replace human effort, an optimistic perspective embraces it as a tool for empowerment. Generative AI does not diminish human creativity; rather, it enhances it by automating repetitive tasks, providing inspiration, and allowing individuals to focus on higher-order thinking. By maintaining a positive outlook on technological advancements, individuals can harness AI's potential to drive innovation rather than resist change.

3. Generative AI as a Reflection of Human Potential

Generative AI is, in many ways, a reflection of human potential itself. It is built upon human intelligence, trained on vast datasets, and designed to simulate creativity. This technology exemplifies how human ingenuity can be encoded into algorithms, demonstrating that even machines can learn to generate novel and meaningful content.

One of the most promising aspects of Generative AI is its collaborative potential. Rather than functioning as a replacement for human effort, AI serves as a co-creator, working alongside individuals to enhance productivity and creativity. In fields such as design, literature, and scientific research, AI-driven tools are enabling humans to accomplish more in less time, pushing the boundaries of innovation.

However, the effectiveness of Generative AI depends on how it is approached. A mindset of optimism encourages individuals to view AI as an asset rather than a threat. By fostering a culture of collaboration between human intelligence and artificial intelligence, the world can unlock unprecedented levels of progress and creativity.

4. Embracing the Future with an Optimistic Mindset

As technology continues to evolve, so too does the scope of human potential. The development of Generative AI underscores the power of optimism in driving progress. Those who approach the future with a belief in limitless possibilities are the ones who shape it. A pessimistic outlook may lead to stagnation and resistance to change, while optimism fuels the courage to explore new frontiers.

To truly harness human potential, society must cultivate a mindset that embraces challenges as opportunities and views technology as a tool for empowerment. Just as past generations used breakthroughs in science and engineering to improve lives, today's advancements in AI present a chance to redefine the future. With optimism as the driving force, humanity can continue to expand its capabilities, proving that the only real limits are those imposed by the mind.

About The Author

Mr. Rakesh Kumar holds a **B.Tech in Computer Science Engineering from RGPV University, Bhopal,** and brings over three years of **experience in technical writing**. He has **contributed to more than 10 books** on cutting-edge topics like **Generative AI, Machine Learning, and Deep Learning**. His writing style is known for breaking down complex concepts into clear, accessible language for readers at all levels.

Driven by a strong passion for technology and innovation, Rakesh created *Mastering Generative AI: A Practical Guide to Machine Learning and Deep Learning* to help readers explore how these transformative technologies are reshaping industries and influencing everyday life. His aim is to bridge the gap between theory and real-world application, making advanced AI concepts practical and relevant.

Beyond writing, Rakesh is an avid **chess player** and a dedicated advocate for disability awareness. Living with a **physical handicap in both legs**, he firmly believes in the power of perseverance, knowledge, and inclusivity. This book reflects his mission to make Generative AI, Machine Learning, and Deep Learning education empowering and accessible to all.

www.ingramcontent.com/pod-product-compliance
Lightning Source LLC
LaVergne TN
LVHW051445050326
832903LV00030BD/3243